3 1994 01326 0317

03/06
2²/07 (12/07)

P9-DVI-138

D

The life of Richard Strauss

Musical lives

Each book in this series provides an account
of the life of a major composer, considering
both the private and the public figure. The
main thread is biographical, and discussion
of the music is integral to the narrative. Each
volume thus presents an organic view of the
composer, the music, and the circumstances
in which the music was written.

Published titles

The life of Richard Strauss

B RYAN G ILLIAM

CAMBRIDGE
UNIVERSITY PRESS

PUBLISHED BY THE PRESS SYNDICATE OF THE UNIVERSITY OF CAMBRIDGE
The Pitt Building, Trumpington Street, Cambridge, United Kingdom

CAMBRIDGE UNIVERSITY PRESS
The Edinburgh Building, Cambridge, CB2 2RU, UK   http://www.cup.cam.ac.uk
40 West 20th Street, New York, NY 10011-4211, USA   http://www.cup.org
10 Stamford Road, Oakleigh, Melbourne 3166, Australia

First published 1999

Printed in the United Kingdom at the University Press, Cambridge

Typeset in FF Quadraat 9.75/14 pt, in QuarkXPress™   [SE]

A catalogue record for this book is available from the British Library

Library of Congress cataloguing in publication data

Gilliam, Bryan Randolph.
The life of Richard Strauss / Bryan Gilliam.
        p.   cm. – (Musical lives)
Includes bibliographical references and index.
ISBN 0 521 57019 0 (hardback). – ISBN 0 521 57895 7 (paperback)
1. Strauss, Richard, 1864–1949.   2. Composers – Germany – Biography.
1. Title.   II. Series.
ML410.S93G53   1999
780'.92–dc21   98-47947   CIP
[b]

ISBN 0 521 57019 0 hardback
ISBN 0 521 57895 7 paperback

CONTENTS

ILLUSTRATIONS

Richard Strauss Archive (RSA) documents were provided, with permission, by the Strauss family. Grateful thanks are due to all copyright
holders.

ACKNOWLEDGMENTS

Without the generous assistance and advice from many friends and colleagues this book would never have appeared. Although Franz Trenner is no longer alive, his spirit of generosity lives on with his family, especially his wife Annelies and their son Florian, who continued to make available Trenner's notes and materials as well as decades of copious notes by his friend Willi Schuh, whose materials were passed on to Trenner after his death. Florian is completing his father's final project, a Diarium of Strauss's entire life, and I was able to consult the drafts so that I might corroborate dates and places. For over twenty years now the Strauss family has shown me nothing but warm and generous hospitality, first Alice Strauss, then and after her passing, Richard and Gabrielle Strauss, and Christian and Susann Strauss. It has been a continuing relationship of cooperation and friendship. I am also grateful to Hartmut Schaeffer and the Bavarian State Library as well as Günter Brosche at the Austrian National Library, also to Reinhold and Roswitha Schlötterer and the Richard Strauss Seminar at the University of Munich. Thanks are also due to so many other friends who have read partial or entire drafts of this volume: Thomas Hansen, Charles Youmans, Pamela Potter, Bill Bonnell, Brian Kileff, and Fred Raimi. I am also grateful to Michael Kater, Susan Gillespie, and Walter Niedermann for their important assistance and advice. Finally, thanks to my wife, who painstakingly went through every page of this manuscript; her unfailing enthusiasm was invaluable during the entire process and I dedicate this book to her.

For Vivian

Introduction

Richard Strauss poses a unique challenge in modern music. His predilection for mixing the trivial and the sublime, for undercutting the extraordinary with the everyday, defies our stereotype of nineteenth- and twentieth-century composers. Indeed, Strauss embodies a fundamental dichotomy that will be a recurring focus in this study of the man and his music. Strauss's world was one clearly divided into two distinct but frequently overlapping spheres of professional and domestic life. Beyond these two spheres, Strauss showed little interest: he had no time for Wagnerian philandering, no space for Brucknerian religious piety, no patience with the insecurities that haunted Mahler, no understanding of the jealousies that plagued Schoenberg. Where other composers derived their creative spark through struggle or personal tragedy, Strauss would simply not indulge. He did not see discipline, order, and stability as obstacles but rather as catalysts for creativity. He once said of Wagner, whose music he admired most of his life, that the brain that composed *Tristan und Isolde* was surely as "cool as marble." It is a statement that says far more about Strauss than Wagner in its emphasis on technique over emotion.

Hans von Bülow once dubbed young Strauss as Richard III (because, after Wagner, there could be no direct successor), but that very persistent focus on Strauss as post-Wagnerian has obscured the fact that the role model for Strauss the man was more likely Johannes

Brahms, whom he met at a crucial time in his life. Brahms, whose rise to prominence coincided with the rise of Viennese liberalism, cultivated a bourgeois image; his apartment was neat and orderly, his books, manuscripts, and printed scores were arranged with remarkable precision. As a composer who was born in the 1830s, Brahms's bourgeois-artist persona was in consonance with its time, but for a creative individual of Strauss's generation the duality of bourgeois and artist was one of increasing conflict. Here is where Strauss stood apart from his contemporaries, for – to the contrary – he saw no such conflict as he eagerly embraced the bourgeoisie of a new generation. The culture industry that was in its infancy during the days of Brahms had come into fruition by the early twentieth century, and no one recognized this phenomenon any better than Strauss, the most successful composer of his time.

On one level Strauss remains one of the most often performed, widely recorded composers of our century, and seems therefore to be readily accessible. Yet on another level we inevitably confront a private, contradictory human being who seems to elude our grasp. Was Strauss a man deeply rooted in inner antagonisms, or did he merely wear several masks? How, indeed, does one come to terms with the creator of temporally adjacent works such as *Symphonia domestica*, with its harmless depiction of family life, and *Salome*, an opera that combines oriental exoticism and sexual depravity? How do we reconcile the avid Bavarian card player with the man of letters who quoted Goethe with ease? What do we make of a composer who, in *Krämerspiegel*, warned that art remains vulnerable to crass business interests, yet who himself conducted concerts at Wanamaker's department store in New York? And, especially important, how does one understand the artist who claimed to embrace Wagner, yet in practice seemed to reject him?

Strauss, the master skat player, kept those cards close to his chest at the table and also in life; he was aloof and seemingly phlegmatic in public, yet extroverted and sanguine in his music. The composer who seems to reveal so much of himself in his works loathed real self-revelation beyond the purely musical realm. Averse to the neo-Romantic posture of the artist set apart from worldly life, Strauss cultivated the image of a composer who treated composition as everyday work, as a way of merely earning an income. But however true this persona may have been on one level, it was no less a pose, a mask so real to others that he could disappear behind it, allowing Strauss the artist his necessary seclusion for creative work. In short, no one was more aware of this man-vs.-artist (the bourgeois-artist) paradox than Strauss himself. He was, after all, the composer who, as memoirs and documentary film footage show, enjoyed conducting his most moving musical passages with minimal body gestures and with a face devoid of emotion.

As a modernist, Strauss also realized the inability of contemporary art to maintain a unified mode of expression. From *Don Juan* to *Der Rosenkavalier* and beyond, Strauss reveled in creating moments of grandeur only to undercut them – sometimes in the most jarring fashion. Unlike Mahler or Schoenberg, who both held to a Romantic view of music as a transcendent, redemptive force, Strauss confronted the problem of modernity head on and came to his own idiosyncratic conclusions. Thus, in a paradoxical way, Strauss exploited a Wagnerian musical language to criticize a metaphysical philosophy behind that very language. His attraction to Nietzsche stemmed from a fundamental desire to debunk the metaphysics of Schopenhauer, specifically the denial of the Will (that primal, unknowable, life force) through music.[1] All life is suffering, according to Schopenhauer, and that primal, metaphysical drive could either be quieted through aesthetic contemplation or entirely negated through an ascetic, Parsifal-like saintliness. Strauss, who had no interest in saintliness or redemption through music, embraced Nietzsche who transformed Schopenhauer's fatalistic "will to life" into an celebratory "will to power." Nietzsche, in short, sought to affirm the very life that Schopenhauer sought to deny, and he also provided the effective apparatus for Strauss's joyful – and life-long – agnosticism in the 1890s.

In an essay written shortly before his death, Strauss lamented (in unmistakably Nietzschean terms) that this aspect of modernity – the recognition of an unbreachable gap between the individual and the collective – went largely unnoticed in his works dating back to the 1890s.[2] In his late essay, Strauss refers to this dichotomy in Act III of *Guntram*, though it could apply as easily to such tone poems as *Also sprach Zarathustra*. Indeed, in a sketch to the opening of this symphonic work, Strauss writes: "The sun rises. The individual enters the world, or the world enters the individual." Strauss's late essay also implies disappointment that for a younger generation of composers a different view of modernism had emerged – one that prized technical progressivity, whereby musical style was viewed as an obligatory, linear process along the axis of tonality–atonality. This Schoenbergian notion of an organic, unified stylistic evolution (with its obvious German-Romantic roots) was alien to Strauss, who recognized, if anything, a profound disunity in modern life and saw no reason that music should be any different. Strauss treated musical style in an ahistorical, often critical fashion that arguably prefigured trends of the late twentieth century. He seems to foreshadow what Fredric Jameson calls the postmodern "collapse of the ideology of style." For Schoenberg and his high-modernist followers there was an implicit perception of "aesthetic immorality" in composing contemporary music in a tonal idiom that was viewed as outworn and moribund. This moralistic aesthetic continued until well after World War II and could merge in and out of a political discourse with remarkable inconsistency, where composers such as Stravinsky or Webern, who enjoyed an aesthetically moral high ground, were forgiven various political sins or had their views misrepresented altogether.

Historians of music often look for an inner unity in a composer's repertoire and, in turn, in the broader connection between that repertoire and the composer's Age. Scholars who have studied the music dramas of Richard Wagner or the symphonies of Gustav Mahler along such lines have been richly rewarded. Yet, the extensive Straussian *œuvre* – which shows a composer equally at ease in the concert hall, recital hall, ballet, cinema, and opera house – is far more resistant to cultural biographers in this respect. Strauss once suggested that his body of work was one "bridged by contrasts," and, indeed, there are hardly two adjacent works that continue in the same mode: tragic or comic. *Ein Heldenleben* is preceded by the anti-heroic *Don Quixote*, and the hyper-symbolic *Frau ohne Schatten* is followed by the light sex-comedy, *Intermezzo*. But in exploring these contrasts one finds intriguing connections: the two tone poems probe and critique heroism in its various guises, while the two operas explore domestic relationships on both mundane and metaphysical levels. Indeed, if there is a significant consistency in Strauss's compositional output, it is in his desire to suggest the profundities and ambiguities to be found in everyday life, even in the apparently banal. The sublime final trio of *Der Rosenkavalier* is based, after all, on a trivial waltz tune heard earlier in the opera.

But beyond all the contrasts, paradoxes, and incongruities there is indeed a coherent shape to be found in Strauss's compositions. His output begins with a focus on lieder and purely instrumental composition: solo piano and chamber music at first, then orchestral music by the 1880s. Toward the end of the decade, he becomes preoccupied with the narrative potential of symphonic music and by the turn of the century, after an intense exploration of the tone poem, Strauss moves on to the stage, and opera remains his principal preoccupation over the remaining decades. Yet after *Capriccio* (1941), the elderly Strauss bade farewell to the theater and returned to those instrumental musical genres of his youth. And there were, of course, the lieder that wove their way throughout Strauss's career at various critical junctures, from the naive youthful pieces to the exalted orchestral songs at the very end of his life.

The ideal likeness of Strauss would not be a painting, drawing, or sculpture; rather, it would be a mosaic: coherent from afar, but upon closer view made of contrasting fragments. Those who shared this closer perspective have, in fact, offered conflicting images of the man: generous, petty, folksy, snobbish, visionary, provincial, tasteless, refined. His was a complex personality that seemed to offer itself to the world without a filtering mechanism. Yet this may well have been the ultimate filter: the pretense of being unpretentious. In *Ariadne auf Naxos* Strauss set compelling music to the words, "music is a sacred art," but he was the same composer who simultaneously insisted that, in capitalism, music is also a commodity, knowing full well the shock value of such a statement.

Strauss would ultimately argue that it was not his job to create a unified picture of himself. When Stefan Zweig, his one-time librettist, suggested that the composer might write an autobiography, Strauss declined stating that he preferred simply to "provide some signposts and then leave it to the scholars to fill in." The composer, thus, invites us to discover whatever there is to learn about him through his music: the cheap and the precious, the commonplace and the sublime. The key may not be to reconcile or resolve such contradictions, but rather to look at them in a dialectical way. What follows are six chapters that cover his early musical development, his emergence as a tone poet in the 1880s and 90s, his turn to the stage at the beginning of the twentieth century, the successes and misfires of the post-World War I era, the turbulent 1930s (a time of artistic and political crisis), and, of course, the period during the Second World War and its aftermath.

1 Musical development and early career

To enter the Strauss villa in Garmisch, home of the composer, is to be confronted by paradox. This house, built in 1908 with the royalties from the sensational *Salome*, was the composer's refuge, a place where the world-weary traveler could return to normalcy. Yet the Garmisch home of this man who visited all the major cities of Europe, who toured North and South America and the Middle East, is anything but international in flavor. A quintessential Bavarian Landhaus, every corner of this mountain retreat exudes the aura of Southern Germany. The walls are covered with regional paintings and Bavarian folk art. South German religious icons, Bavarian clocks, and other regional artifacts make an equally strong impression. Could this be the home of the man who eagerly left Bavaria for Prussia in 1898, the man who, two years later, composed an opera mocking Munich philistinism and provinciality? Moreover, given the length and breadth of his cosmo-politan career, which city could claim him as its own? Berlin, where he served as music director to the Court Opera and Orchestra during his twenty most productive years; Dresden, the composer's "glückliche Stadt" which saw more Strauss opera premieres than any other; Vienna, where he co-directed the State Opera from 1919 to 1924 and where he built his impressive mansion at the edge of the Belvedere; or his native Munich? And what about Switzerland, where Strauss spent his final post-war years in the various hotels of Zurich, Lucerne, and Montreux?

Strauss was born in 1864 a Bavarian, a subject of the castle-building King Ludwig II, who was crowned just three months before his birth. Bavarian independence was in its final phase, and seven years later, in the wake of the Franco-Prussian War, a reluctant Ludwig would yield political authority to Wilhelm I, King of Prussia and Emperor of the Second German Empire. Still, even after the formation of the empire, Ludwig's image in Bavaria would be felt and would indirectly shape the lives of both Richard and his father, Franz Strauss. The eccentric Ludwig was Wagner's most famous patron, and he brought the debt-ridden composer to Munich, where he would reside, albeit briefly, under royal protection. Although Wagner's actual stay in Munich amounted to only some eighteen months, his presence lingered in the Bavarian capital for decades to come. For good or bad, the Wagnerian aura would play a central role for Strauss as a maturing artist.

Richard's father, Franz, detested Wagner, though he played first horn for the premieres of *Tristan und Isolde, Die Meistersinger, Das Rheingold, Die Walküre,* and *Parsifal*. Wagner and Hans von Bülow were dumbfounded that such an unsympathetic musician could play the difficult horn parts with such skill and nuance.[1] Indeed, Franz's irascibility was surpassed only by his talent, something that Wagner and Bülow (who dubbed him the "Joachim of the horn") soon came to accept. Reminiscing in his later years, Richard would describe his father as "a character," but a person, nevertheless, to be taken seriously, for Franz was the first and most important musical figure in Strauss's early life, an influence whose power and influence cannot be overestimated. Struggle and hardship were practically all that Franz knew before he married Josephine Pschorr in 1863 when he was forty-one. A year later she gave birth to a baby boy described by the ecstatic father as "healthy, pretty, and round as a ball." If Franz Strauss's exuberance was more than that of the typical new parent, it was understandable, for he had lost his first wife and two children to tuberculosis and cholera between the years 1852 and 1854. Richard's birth represented a second chance at establishing a family for Franz, who would see the birth of a daughter, Johanna, three years later.

Franz Strauss was born out of wedlock in 1822, and though his father, Urban, acknowledged him as his son and gave him his surname, he neither married the mother, Kunigunda Walter, nor assumed any responsibilities in raising him. Urban moved away after five years, ultimately marrying another woman who bore him five children; he maintained no contact with his illegitimate offspring. The paternal void would be filled by Kunigunda's brothers, Johann Georg, a freelance musician, and Franz Michael Walter, a tower master in Nabburg, a small town in the Oberpfalz, roughly fifty miles east of Nuremberg. Music making was an essential part of life for the versatile Walter family. Johann was an accomplished horn player, and tower master Franz Michael not only had to play the hourly trumpet signal but was also in charge of maintaining the Nabburg parish band. Both uncles augmented their meager income as journeymen musicians and they, necessarily, played a remarkable variety of instruments.

Musical versatility was the key to survival, and they transferred this reality to Franz who, as a young boy, learned guitar, violin, clarinet, and various brass instruments. Uncle Johann also taught Franz basic theory and rudimentary composition, and by the time Franz was ten, he was soon traveling with his uncles for their various musical engagements (weddings, fairs, and dances), and also earning income by offering private music lessons. At age fifteen Franz found himself, with the help of his uncles, in the employ of Duke Maximilian, cousin of King Ludwig I. As a court musician to the duke he played guitar, but all the while Franz was becoming increasingly proficient on the French horn, his Uncle Georg's favorite instrument. Within ten years Franz Strauss would join the Munich Court Orchestra as horn player and occasional violist. However, it was the French horn that would become his stepladder out of poverty.

Franz was a superb musician whose brilliance was equaled only by his dogged tenacity. Though devastated by the loss of his wife and children in the early 1850s, a hardened Strauss was nonetheless determined to prevail: he joined the court orchestra in 1847, soon working

1 Franz Strauss near the end of his life: father and musical
mentor, world-renowned horn player

his way to first horn. He was appointed Professor at the Königliche
Musikshule (Royal Music School) in 1871 and was named Kammer-
musiker, a distinguished honorary title, only two years later. With the
marriage to Josephine Pschorr, after seven years of courtship, Franz
had achieved something that neither his mother nor his uncles had
ever dreamed of, namely entry into the middle class. Though the
Pschorr family fortune came from brewing beer, they were a large,
music-loving family. Performing music was an important and regular
part of family life, but it was still an avocation. Never before had a pro-

fessional musician joined the family, and father Georg Pschorr was initially ambivalent about such a union. There was possibly a deeper reason for the father's ambivalence, a reason that would have likely not been openly discussed: Josephine had a nervous disorder, a problem that got worse as she aged. Georg might well have wondered how such a relationship, between the strong, outspoken Franz and the quiet, nervous Josephine, would play out.

The tenacious Strauss prevailed and finally won over the skeptical brewing magnate and was welcomed into the family, in 1863, with genuine warmth. Franz and Josephine moved into an apartment on the second floor of the back of the Pschorr brewery (Altheimereck 2), where Richard was born a year later. Thus, the young composer would grow up in the heart of the Bavarian capital, whose population at the time numbered some 150,000 inhabitants. Young Strauss would be able to capitalize on all that a metropolis had to offer – theaters, concert halls, museums – and, of course, through his father, he would make early contacts with Munich's most important musicians. His earliest musical experience beyond the family home was military music, but unlike the martial music that fascinated young Gustav Mahler, who grew up near military barracks in Iglau (Moravia), Strauss's music came from the midday changing of the guard on the Marienplatz. There, in the town house of his wealthy great-grandmother, the three-year-old Strauss would watch from her window. Afterwards, he would imitate playing the drum on the way home, and much to his father's amazement, he would sometimes play a military tune on the piano from memory. Within four years Strauss would begin seeing his first operas (*Die Zauberflöte* and *Der Freischütz*) and by age eight he started attending symphony concerts regularly, eagerly watching his father leading the horn section.

Though the precocious young Strauss would soon be named as Wagner's legitimate successor by Hans von Bülow, his musical upbringing contrasted remarkably with that of the elder composer, whose roots were firmly planted in the world of the theater. From the beginning, Wagner's music was an extension of the dramatic impulse whereas Strauss's formative roots, which were set in a strict, conservative tradition emphasizing instrumental music and lieder, in no way pointed towards the career of a composer who would ultimately produce fifteen operas, outnumbering even Wagner himself. If anything, Strauss's bourgeois upbringing and classical training, where domestic music-making played a vital role in family life, suggests far more similarities with Wagner's putative antipode, Felix Mendelssohn. Strauss certainly preferred Mendelssohn to Wagner as a young boy, and his love for the composer continued long after he assumed the mantle of *Zukunftmusiker*.

Like Mendelssohn, Strauss was a remarkable prodigy. He began playing the piano by age three and started formal lessons with Munich Court Orchestra harpist August Tombo a year later. Also like Mendelssohn, Strauss had an exceptionally musically literate father who was both highly opinionated and arch-conservative: indeed, neither Abraham Mendelssohn nor Franz Strauss could tolerate even late Beethoven. Though motivated by different reasons, Franz Strauss, like father Abraham, wanted his son to have a strong liberal arts education, one that would provide a firm and broad foundation, emphasizing literature, history, Greek, and Latin. The thought of young Richard attending a conservatory was out of the question, much to the son's annoyance, for father Franz knew all too well the realities of depending on music as the sole means for survival. He was determined that his son would not enter the musical world at an unripe age as he had. Richard began the Ludwigsgymnasium at age ten, yet by then he had already established himself as a precocious musician. His first two compositions (the *Schneiderpolka* for piano and the *Weihnachtslied* for soprano), both written at age six, suggested the two basic directions in his early compositional career, instrumental composition and lieder.

Franz Strauss wanted to nurture the artistic side of his son's personality while simultaneously preparing the young boy for modern bourgeois life. Thus, Richard the musician was to develop in the seclusion of rigorous, private study, but would receive his intellectual training at the Gymnasium. Entry into grammar school was balanced with more intensive piano study with Carl Niest and, more importantly, compositional studies with Friedrich Wilhelm Meyer, from whom he would learn harmony, counterpoint, musical form, and ultimately orchestration. As an assistant to Franz Lachner, Hofkapellmeister to the court, Meyer maintained a relatively low profile in the Munich musical scene, where he conducted the operas that did not interest Lachner: Auber, Donizetti, Boieldieu, and the like. Years later his most famous pupil would describe the modestly gifted Meyer as a "simple man with a noble mind," but why would Franz Strauss choose someone so lacking in brilliance for his brilliant son? Surely by the 1870s Franz had attained a level of influence in Munich that would have allowed him to ask any number of the most influential musical figures in the city. But father Strauss wanted to maintain control over his son's progress; he wanted a conservative teacher who would be deferential to his wishes, and one who could also give his full attention to his student's progress. The childless Meyer, who treated Richard almost like a son, was ideal, despite the fact that he was not averse to the music of Wagner and Liszt.

There are no known published works by Meyer, and the surviving pieces in manuscript show little originality. Nonetheless, what Franz Strauss foremost admired in Meyer was his distrust of theorists and treatises as a source for teaching composition. Franz, ever the iconoclast and autodidact, had achieved great success in the musical world without methodological, academic training, and he wanted to instill that type of unsystematic musical independence in his son. It should be added that he was largely successful, for one can detect the unmistakable voice of the father in a letter to Ludwig Thuille by the fourteen-year-old Strauss. Thuille had asked Strauss about a composition textbook, and Richard readily offered his, or his father's, opinion:

> So far as learning instrumental music is concerned, I can only give
> you *one* piece of good advice – not to learn it from a book, since this,
> as my father says, is the worst thing. So I advise you not to buy a book,
> since even my papa only knows one by Hector Berlioz, who is a real

2 The composer and his sister, Johanna, in 1873

scribbler and a hack; instead ask Herr Pembaur for a table covering
the range and the best position of the various instruments that are
used and learn the rest, that is, the use and application of the same,
from the scores of the great old masters, which Herr Pembaur, if you
ask Frau Nagiller to lean on him a bit, will surely lend you.[2]

We know from another letter to Thuille that Strauss did indeed use a textbook (Ernst Friedrich Richter's *Grundzüge der musikalischen Formen* [1852]), a brief 52-page theory manual that was intended only as an introduction to musical form and served as a basis for independent study, the very type of study encouraged by both Meyer and Strauss's father. Curiously, a year before Franz's death a far different Richard Strauss paid tribute to the "scribbler and hack" when he published an expanded German edition (by Breitkopf und Härtel) of Berlioz's treatise on orchestration in 1904.

Of all Strauss's childhood acquaintances, Ludwig Thuille was the most influential and beneficial to his early musical development. The slightly older Thuille would prove to be a vital outlet for a boy who had few childhood friends with whom he could discuss music in detail. Though they first met in 1872 (ages eight and eleven, respectively), they did not get to know one another until five years later, when Pauline Nagiller, a widowed friend of Strauss's mother, became Thuille's legal guardian. Thuille was orphaned at an early age, and before being taken in by Nagiller in Innsbruck he was raised by a great-uncle. Franz Strauss, who doubtless identified with the young orphan, treated him as one of the family and helped guide his career. In 1879, Thuille gained admission in the Munich Königliche Musikschule, where Franz taught horn, and there he studied theory and composition with Joseph Rheinberger. A more influential theorist than composer, Thuille would become a leading member of the so-called Munich School. He succeeded Rheinberger in 1903 at the Academy and shortly thereafter collaborated with Rudolf Louis on a *Harmonielehre* (1907) that remained an important theoretical text for decades. The 46-year-old Thuille died of a heart attack the year the work was published.

Thuille was a frequent guest in the Strauss home, where he often took part in domestic music making, and the two boys enjoyed going to concerts together. Much of their early time was spent apart, while Thuille attended the Gymnasium in Innsbruck from 1877 to 1879, but they exchanged numerous letters and critiqued one another's compositions, often in great detail. Unfortunately, the letters from Thuille during the Innsbruck years are lost; however, the abundant letters by Strauss represent the closest thing we have to a childhood diary of the composer, for they constitute a record of his composing, concert-going, and performing. His concert reviews are sometimes quite long, often with musical passages quoted from memory. These reviews reveal the boy's profound regard for the classic masters: Haydn, Beethoven, Schubert, and especially Mozart. But he was also quite fond of Mendelssohn and Schumann, the latter who showed an "inevitable tendency to ride his figures to death." Though Strauss's respect for Weber, Spohr, Lachner, Lortzing, and Marschner is hardly surprising, his youthful enthusiasm for Boieldieu and Auber amused the older Thuille.

Such opinions embarrassed Strauss when he was older, and he was often annoyed at seeing excerpts of this correspondence in print. Even more embarrassing for the composer were the frequent negative youthful comments concerning Wagner such as when he declared that in ten years the Bayreuth master would be long forgotten. But such naive hyperbole should not suggest an ignorance of the composer. Even at age fourteen Strauss could write his friend in Wagnerian alliterative verse:

> Nach langem und sehnlichen, sauren Warten/ hielt in Händen ich endlich die neidliche Post;/ich warte weiland auf Walhalls Zinnen/vor Sehnsucht verzehrte mich beinahe der Rost . . . (Long I listed, in painful delay;/here I hold your mail at last in my fist/woeful I waited on Valhalla's walls,/yearning I was almost devoured by rust . . .)[3]

Despite the fact that these letters are full of digs at *Lohengrin*, which he calls "Lohengelb," or "Lohenyellow,"[4] and at the *Ring*, the accuracy of musical detail suggests an uncommon understanding of Wagner. Indeed, one letter describes a treacherous family mountain expedition, which seems to have sparked an early interest in Wagnerian tone painting, and perhaps even foreshadowed a future alpine symphony: "The next day I described the whole hike on the piano. Naturally huge tone paintings and smarminess à la Wagner. Recently I saw *Götterdämmerung*."[5]

The bond between Strauss and Thuille was a mixture of friendship and rivalry, and later on in the relationship jealousies would inevitably surface, for Thuille was different from Strauss in many ways. More cautious and introverted than his younger companion, he was also admittedly less talented, and it became increasingly difficult for the maturing Thuille to see the brilliant young, sanguine Strauss, who seemed to live in such a comfortable, stable home, without a certain degree of envy. Unaware of Thuille's jealousy, Strauss openly admired his older friend as a musician and a composer. Among other works, he dedicated his *Don Juan* to Thuille, and as late as 1902, while Strauss was in the midst of composing *Symphonia domestica*, he sent Thuille a fugue statement asking him if he could come up with a proper fugal answer as well as a good two-voice counterpoint. As an adult, Thuille went the way of the musical academy (the route that Richard originally wanted to take). Even though Thuille composed operas, chamber music, and symphonic works, his livelihood came from teaching composition. He saw in Strauss a younger, more talented composer – one whose career as a composer was growing at an exponential rate.

The works that Strauss composed during the 1870s were mostly small-scaled and written with specific family members in mind: songs, pieces for solo piano, and chamber music. These early lieder were mostly for his aunt, Johanna Pschorr, a fine mezzo soprano, who would sing them at family musicales. Many of these works are now lost, but those that survive show a young composer well grounded in an early nineteenth-century lied tradition. It is difficult to keep track of Strauss's numerous cousins and the instruments they played. Richard himself especially enjoyed playing chamber music with Ludwig Knözinger, Karl Streicher, and Karl Aschenbrenner. Performing such music stimulated his own composition, though, years later, Strauss observed that he had probably been over-stimulated, that he had written far too many works during the 1870s. Indeed, he would later stipulate in his will that, after his death, these works should never be published or performed.

Toward the end of the 1870s Strauss demonstrated an increasing interest in orchestral music, probably linked to the fact that his father had taken over the so-called Wilde Gung'l Orchestra in 1875. This amateur orchestra, which Franz Strauss led until 1896, helped introduce Richard to the world of symphonic composition. He attended rehearsals and himself joined the ensemble in 1882 as a first violinist. Beyond the teaching of Meyer, the Wilde Gung'l allowed Strauss to learn orchestration on a practical level, his father helping to guide the way, and some of his earliest orchestral pieces were written for this group, which is still in existence. His first orchestral piece, the Concert Overture in B minor (1876), was scored with the help of Meyer, but his *Festmarsch*, completed later that year, was orchestrated entirely by the twelve-year-old composer. A number of other overtures and marches would follow, and even a D minor symphony in 1880. But the best-known works by Strauss from the early 1880s were the Serenade, Op. 7 (1881), the Piano Sonata, Op. 5 (1880–81), the Five Pieces for Piano, Op. 3 (1880–81), and the concerti for violin (1882) and for the horn (1883).

Strauss graduated from the Ludwigsgymnasium and, in accordance with his father's wishes, entered the University of Munich, though ultimately for only the winter semester of 1882–83. A major event during the summer after graduation was Strauss's trip to Bayreuth with his father, who played first horn for the premiere of *Parsifal*. By then Richard had heard all of Wagner's major operas, and, despite his outward protests to the contrary, Wagner's music increasingly fascinated him. In the autumn of 1880, he had, indeed, secretly studied the score to *Tristan*, much to his father's later dismay. But Franz knew that his strong grip on the impatient young composer could not be maintained indefinitely: Richard was eager to make his way into the world of music, and his father knew that by the early 1880s his son was growing musically by leaps and bounds; it was too late to do anything but let him leave the university and move on. Yet as brief as his university study may have been, it should not be over-looked, for in many ways it marked the beginning of Strauss's awak-ening intellectual personality. In his only semester at the Ludwig-Maximilian University he studied Shakespeare, art history, philosophy, and aesthetics – studies that would directly affect his artistic growth over the next decade. While at the university he also became interested in Schopenhauer, whose writings he discussed at length with his classmate Arthur Seidl and with Friedrich Rösch, an old friend from school days.

Meanwhile, Strauss was beginning to make a real name for him-self, for even before leaving the Gymnasium his first symphony had been premiered in 1880 by Hermann Levi in the Odeonsaal to positive reviews. More important was the 1882 premiere of the Op. 7 Woodwind Serenade, a work that reversed Hans von Bülow's early negative opinion of the composer. Bülow's friend Eugen Spitzweg was Strauss's first publisher, from the Munich-based Aibl Verlag, and in 1881 he had solicited the conductor's opinion of the Five Piano Pieces (Op. 3) and the *Stimmungsbilder* (Op. 9): Bülow was hardly moved: "*Do not care* for the piano pieces by Richard Strauss in the least . . . fail to find any signs of youth in his invention. *Not a genius* in my most sincere belief, but at best a talent . . . Pity the piano writing is so clumsy, so much in need of practical improvements."[6] But the *Serenade*, completed in November 1881, changed Bülow's mind, so much so that he agreed to program the work while on tour in Berlin with the Meiningen Orchestra.

Strauss made his first tour as a composer traveling to Vienna in December 1882, where his Violin Concerto was premiered (in a violin–piano arrangement) by his cousin and violin teacher Benno Walter with Eugenie Menter on piano. The eighteen-year-old Strauss was eager to get a sample of Viennese cultural life when the Vienna Court Opera was enjoying unprecedented fame with Wilhelm Jahn in the directorship. Jahn had wisely turned over the German repertoire to Wagner's friend and champion Hans Richter, and, indeed, Strauss was able to see a production of *Tannhäuser* under Richter the day after his arrival in the Austrian capital. The next day he again heard Richter lead the Vienna Philharmonic, this time in a matinee orchestral concert that included Brahms's Serenade in D major. The juxtaposition of Wagner and Brahms takes on greater meaning when one remembers how sharply drawn the battle lines between the "music of the future" and "conservative Romanticism" actually were at that time in Vienna. And one wonders about Strauss's reaction to these adjacent events, away from home and from his cantankerous father who disliked Brahms as much as Wagner. But beneath all his irascibility, Franz knew the politics of music, and he insisted that his 18-year-old son make numerous courtesy calls. Though he failed to meet with Eduard Hanslick (famed music critic for the *Neue freie Presse* and emblem of the Viennese-liberal musical mainstream), he managed to make appointments with Richter and Wilhelm Jahn, and with music critic Max Kalbeck, who was persuaded to write a small feature on Strauss a day before the violin concerto premiere. Days after the premiere Strauss was pleased to read a favorable review written by Hanslick himself: "My first and only compliment from Hanslick," the composer remarked years later. All in all, young Strauss enjoyed being away from home and out in Viennese society, although he claimed that ultimately Vienna was a very normal city, not unlike Munich.

It was not the trip to Vienna, but rather the journey to Berlin, during the winter of 1883–84, that had such a strong impact on the career of this rapidly-maturing composer. Indeed, this extended trip – something of a deferred *Abiturreise* in view of the fact that he ended his formal education with the Gymnasium – was a signal event in the life of the teenage composer on the threshold of independence. Franz Strauss put great hope in his son's trip to the seat of the young German empire, and he supplied his son with various letters of introduction and persuaded other Munich musical luminaries (such as Levi) to do so as well. Young Strauss was enthusiastic and charming and took full advantage of what Berlin had to offer. There he witnessed some of the finest theatrical productions in Germany, and he would attend operas and concerts by some of the world's finest musicians. Yet the three months (21 December 1883 through 29 March 1884) did more than merely broaden his cultural scope: they gave Strauss the opportunity to promote his work and to meet important, influential artists and intellectuals, some of whom would directly affect the shape of his career.

Berlin was Strauss's ultimate goal on this formative trip, but there were some important stops along the way. On 5 December he arrived in Leipzig – the city of Bach and Mendelssohn, and the place where the conservative Carl Reinecke led Mendelssohn's beloved Gewandhaus Orchestra until 1895. Strauss, who had just completed the last movement of his Second Symphony, played it for Reinecke with the hope that the entire symphony would be performed at a future date; he also performed his Concert Overture. But the cautious Reinecke would not commit, and Strauss, who was happy to get out of "grubby and uninteresting" Leipzig, left for Nuremberg, where his Cello Sonata was premiered by Hans (Hanus) Wihan, accompanied by Hildegard von Königsthal. The noted Czech cellist, for whom Dvořák composed his Cello Concerto (1895), was the principal cellist of the Munich Court Orchestra in the early 1880s and a Strauss family friend. His wife, Dora Weis, was herself a gifted pianist and was close to Strauss's sister, Johanna, especially while her marriage to the temperamental, jealous Hans was on shaky ground. After Wihan left Munich for Prague, his wife stayed behind and would come also to rely on Richard for emotional support. The extent of their relationship beyond that has never been substantiated, but they were nonetheless the talk of Munich society until Strauss left for Meiningen in fall 1885.

Dora's parents shared their home with Strauss during his fortnight in Dresden, home of the famed Staatskapelle, which had been recently taken over by Ernst von Schuch. Shortly before Strauss's arrival, the orchestra and opera had been led by Franz Wüllner, who was from Munich and would later premiere some of Strauss's best-known tone poems. Strauss was delighted to see their old family friend Wüllner, who was still in Dresden and would, likewise, be going to Berlin in order to direct the newly organized Philharmonic Orchestra.

Strauss was introduced to von Schuch and he attended rehearsals, and, indeed, while staying with principal cellist Ferdinand Böckmann and his wife, he would imitate von Schuch's conducting technique using a wooden knitting needle. Böckmann, who had just come home from three hours of rehearsing *Tristan*, grabbed the boy's "baton," exclaiming: "My dear Richard, do just stop that! I've had Schuch fumbling about under my nose for three hours today, and I've had enough of it!" Who would have thought in 1883 that Dresden would become the principal site for Strauss's operatic premieres? Beginning in 1901 von Schuch would conduct a string of first performances beginning with *Feuersnot* (1901), then *Salome* (1905), *Elektra* (1909), and *Der Rosenkavalier* (1911); after his death Strauss's *Intermezzo* (1924), *Die ägyptische Helena* (1928), *Arabella* (1933), *Die schweigsame Frau* (1935), and *Daphne* (1938) would premiere there as well. From the very beginning, Strauss loved Dresden: its architecture, its galleries, its museums; and it was a love that only deepened during his long life – a love that turned to utter despair after the city was leveled by fire bombs in 1945.

On 21 December 1883 Strauss left for Berlin, which was rapidly becoming one of the major music centers in the world. Numerous excellent private orchestras flourished there around the middle of the nineteenth century (Orchesterverein Euterpe, Bilsesche Kapelle) and by 1882 a Philharmonic Orchestra (later the Berlin Philharmonic) was founded with Wüllner as its first music director, although he was succeeded by Joseph Joachim a year later. Violinist, composer, and conductor, Joachim was Brahms's lifelong friend and advisor; his magnetic presence in Berlin was strongly felt and attracted some of Europe's finest musicians to the Prussian capital. Indeed, Strauss met with Joachim within five days of his Berlin arrival and stayed in contact with him throughout his visit. But there was an aspect to this Berlin trip far more important than the concerts, introductions, the socializing, and that was the emergence of Strauss as an artistic individual beyond the orbit of his powerful father.

A careful reading of his letters to his parents during the Berlin period reveals a process of subtle and gradual detachment. Throughout his early life Strauss, though oftentimes brash, wanted to please those around him; his letters and comments must always be understood within this context. The same is true of his relationship to his father: wanting to please him on one level, yet wanting go his own way on another. His experience with Brahms's Third Symphony just two weeks into his Berlin stay illustrates this point. After a dress rehearsal under Joachim he wrote to his father that his head was "still reeling from its lack of clarity." He goes on: "I say in all honesty that I don't yet understand it; it is scored so miserably and unclearly . . . Of course, you can't say that here because Joachim, etc., all enthuse over Brahms."[7] Papa Strauss was no doubt doubly pleased: first, that he was not seduced by the Brahmsian side and, second, that he held his tongue (a frequent paternal admonishment in these letters). Yet by the end of the month Strauss was clearly weakening. He attended another rehearsal of the Third on 28 January followed by the concert on the next day, which also featured Brahms playing his own First Piano Concerto. He revealed his change of heart to his father on 1 February:

> This symphony (F major) is one of the most beautiful, original, and fresh that Brahms has ever created. Under [Brahms's] able direction, the orchestra played dashingly. Also he played his D minor concerto with great execution and verve. The concerto is not as fresh and original as the symphony, but on the whole quite interesting.[8]

In a letter to Thuille, Strauss even confessed to becoming "very attached" to Brahms: "He is always interesting and very often really beautiful as well." Only a day after the Brahms concert, Strauss went to hear a performance of *Tristan*. In that same February letter to his father Strauss writes a curious critique, one that can only be understood in the context of this complex and evolving relationship between father and son. Trying hard to criticize a work that obviously fascinates him, he describes *Tristan* as "heavy fare" except for the prelude and introduction to Act I, the potion scene, the opening of Act II and the ensuing love duet, the opening of Act III, and the *Liebestod*. Beyond these remarkably lengthy exceptions, he likens the rest to foods that one would not wish for a steady diet: salmon with remoulade, lobster and mayonnaise. The piquant harmonies at first delight the ear, but one is soon overfed by the pervasive dissonance and chromaticism.

The work of Brahms and Wagner, two composers alien to the Munich Strauss household, was becoming increasingly a part of Strauss's artistic consciousness, though their music was not yet noticeable in the young man's composition. That musical awareness was to be further stimulated by his acquaintance and ultimate friendship with Franz Strauss's enemy, Hans von Bülow, the early champion of Wagner's works who, by the 1880s, had become a stalwart proponent of Brahms. Of all the musicians Strauss met in Berlin, Bülow made the strongest impression, and though he admired Bülow's "phrasing, touch, and execution" as a pianist, it was Bülow the conductor who so strongly affected the young composer. Strauss was astonished that this man not only conducted concerts from memory but rehearsals as well, and though he was not entirely won over at first, Strauss was soon captivated by Bülow's probing interpretations of orchestral music – he also intensified Strauss's growing interest in the work of Brahms. We know from his reaction to the early piano pieces that Bülow was hardly an early convert to the young Strauss, and we can also recall that it was only after Strauss's friend and first publisher Eugen Spitzweg sent a copy of the Serenade to Bülow that he changed his mind about Strauss and scheduled a performance of the Serenade for December 1883. Bülow and his Meiningen Orchestra, a modest group that he turned into one of the great German orchestral ensembles, toured Berlin in February, when the Serenade was once again performed – this time with the composer in the audience. Bülow was so pleased with the result that he commissioned from Strauss another woodwind piece (the Suite in B♭ Major) to be performed by the Meiningen group the following fall.

Shortly after the premiere of his modest Concert Overture by the Berlin Court Orchestra, Strauss left for home, rejoined his father's

Wilde Gung'l Orchestra and returned to serious composing. But now his work was at last to be informed and tempered by the spirit of Brahms. The first product of his so-called "Brahmsschwärmerei" was not a symphony, concerto, or piece of chamber music, rather a six-part choral work (*Wandrers Sturmlied*) that was based on a recently composed work by Brahms that he had heard while in Leipzig on his way to Berlin: the *Gesang der Parzen* (1882), which used a text by Goethe. Similarly, Strauss chose Goethe of his *Sturm und Drang* period, a text that was conceived as the poet wandered through a storm thinking of his former love, Frederike Brion. The poem, an imitation of a Pindaric ode, is full of flashes of insight and sharply juxtaposed images, as well as abundant classical allusions. The portion that Strauss set tells us much about the composer's early religious-philosophical tendencies and contains themes that weave their way throughout Strauss's later life. Tellingly, the Wanderer asks not God but rather his Genius to protect him from the storm, for to Strauss's thinking (even at age nineteen) the divine is only to be found in humanity's ideas and deeds, in inspiration and the work that it inspires. Protected by Genius, the Wanderer ultimately hovers above the earth like the gods themselves (*göttergleich*).

Strauss was agnostic by his mid-teens and he remained so until the end of his life. Even months before his death, the composer declared: "I shall never be converted, and I will remain true to my old religion of the classics until my life's end!" But what was the source of Strauss's indifference toward Christianity, especially given the fact that he grew up in the most devoutly Roman Catholic region of Germany? The Strauss family, though of course Catholics, did not practice the Roman Catholicism predominant in Southern Germany. In his typically iconoclastic way, Franz Strauss rejected the Roman Church and embraced the so-called Old Catholic movement in the early 1870s. This movement was a small sect centered in South Germany, and one that, most importantly, refused to recognize Vatican I's establishment of papal infallibility. Their Old Catholic Mass was conducted in the vernacular, confession was not required, nor were priests required

to be celibate. Very little is known about Richard's religious upbringing, he rarely mentions religion in his youthful letters, but there is no
evidence to suggest that his parents in any way tried to reverse their
son's irreligious leanings. For Strauss, music – its inspiration and its
process – was spiritual sustenance enough. He once remarked to his
schoolmate and future biographer Max Steinitzer that the only spiritual uplift he got from Bach's religious music was from the ingenious
counterpoint. As we shall see in the next chapter, Strauss's anti-
metaphysical leanings would complicate his so-called "conversion"
to the aesthetics and philosophies of Wagner and Liszt.

Only three days after his return from Berlin to Munich Strauss
attended a concert of *Parsifal* excerpts, which he declared to be
"boring," yet curiously there are hints of the opera to be found in the
mostly Brahmsian *Sturmlied*, especially the Good Friday-like final section as the chorus sings the word "göttergleich." The spring and
summer of 1884 were relatively uneventful, save for the fact that he
was composing steadily: some songs and, more importantly, the
Piano Quartet in C minor, a work modeled on Brahms's piano quartet
of the same key. But the main project that summer was writing the
woodwind Suite in B♭ that Bülow had commissioned for Meiningen; it
was completed by the early fall. The premiere (18 November 1884) was
important as it marked Strauss's debut as a conductor – by all
accounts one of the most unusual conducting debuts of all time. As
Strauss later reminisced:

> In the winter of 1884 Bülow came to Munich and surprised me, when
> I visited him, by informing me that he would give a matinée
> performance before an invited audience . . . the program of which
> was to contain as its second item my Suite for Woodwinds, which I
> was to conduct. I thanked him, overjoyed, but told him that I had
> never had a baton in my hand before and asked him when I could
> rehearse. "There will be no time for rehearsals, the orchestra has no
> time for such things on tour" . . . The matinée took its course. I
> conducted my piece in a state of slight coma; I can only remember
> today that I made no blunders.[9]

Encouraged by Bülow, Strauss sent a copy of the score, along with a letter, to Brahms for his comments. His reaction was, on the whole, positive; Brahms praised his technical abilities but found Strauss somewhat wanting in the creation of good melodies, a criticism which would again surface when they had their first meeting a year later.

Brahms's misgivings notwithstanding, the 21-year-old Strauss was well on his way toward international fame. Within a month of Strauss's Munich conducting debut, his Second Symphony received its world premiere in New York City, under the baton of Theodor Thomas, who had earlier been traveling through Europe looking for young talent. After reading through the score with Strauss, the enthusiastic Thomas promised, on the spot, a performance with his New York Philharmonic Society. The German premiere followed a month later (13 January 1885) in Cologne under Wüllner. On the surface things seemed as if they could not be better: successful premieres in New York and Cologne, followed shortly thereafter by the premiere of his Horn Concerto in Meiningen. But a family crisis cast a shadow on Strauss's recent triumphs. His mother, Josephine, was institutionalized in the famous sanatorium in Eglfing on 14 April and was not allowed any visitors until early May. The town of Eglfing, with its famous sanatorium, lay just outside Munich and became better known as the place where Ludwig II would be institutionalized some years later.

Though there is little to document, the effect of Josephine's mental illness on Strauss's personality should not be underestimated. Indeed, beyond the obvious socio-economic differences, Strauss's upbringing was closer to that of Gustav Mahler than many biographers care to emphasize. One biographer, Herta Blaukopf, for example, tried to find stark contrasts in the childhood upbringing of Mahler's unstable and Strauss's supposedly stable youth to explain why "Mahler developed into the harbinger of suffering . . . Strauss into the bestower of joy."[10] Yet, economics aside, we know that both composers had overbearing, sometimes tyrannical, fathers with wives who, all too often, suffered in silence, or without support. Josephine had, in fact, to be institutionalized on various occasions, sometimes for one month, sometimes as long as ten and a half. One wonders indeed what emotional realities lurked behind young Richard's façade of cheerfulness and stability – a façade that both Franz and Richard's sister, Johanna, increasingly came to depend on. In a rare moment, on 25 April 1885, Strauss confided in his sister:

> My optimism and spirits seem to be slipping gradually, there's a limit to everything, I'm afraid, and when I pull myself together as best I can and comfort Papa, it's a waste of time trying to distract him – that's the saddest thing – he's becoming more and more unsociable, I think he feels he's doing dear Mama a moral wrong of some kind if he allows himself to be distracted and doesn't sit all day brooding on our misfortune . . . I hope you're in no doubt that I do everything possible to demonstrate my loyalty and devotion to Papa, I do the best I can to work off some part of the immense debt I owe him in these circumstances, and I hope my resolution will hold out until you come home.[11]

The final sentence, of course, proclaims a vital difference between Strauss and Mahler, for despite Franz's temper and vehemence, Richard deeply admired his difficult artist-father throughout his life, and though he had his mother's sensitivity, he shared his father's utter devotion to work. Franz's brooding, suggested in Richard's letter, was uncharacteristic and momentary. On the whole, his career showed a personality that refused to dwell on the negative, one that believed suffering and grief to be private matters that should not be a source for self-indulgence. It is significant that Franz never spoke to Richard either about the hardships of his youth or about the fact that his first family had been wiped out by sickness within two years during the early 1850s. Franz was convinced that, through a dedication to work, one could overcome most anything.

If the agnostic Richard believed in anything, it was the spiritual nature of inspiration and work, a position that put him at odds with his colleague and friend Gustav Mahler. Strauss could hardly have

3 Gustav Mahler: composer, conductor, and Strauss's friendly rival

imagined what it was like to be in the skin of this secular-mystical Jew who sought redemption from his race and background through conversion and, more importantly, through composing. Socially and spiritually, Strauss and Mahler lived in mutually exclusive worlds. Shortly after Mahler's death in 1911, Strauss pondered the composer's preoccupation with redemption. "I don't know what I am supposed to be redeemed from," Strauss purportedly stated. "When I sit at my desk in the morning and an idea comes into my head, I surely don't need redemption."[12] No doubt, Strauss enjoyed the shock effect of this statement, but by then he firmly believed that music ultimately could not redeem, heal, or transport. In the mind of the 21-year-old Strauss, however, these ideas were still inchoate and would not begin to crystallize until he left home, in autumn 1885, to become Bülow's assistant in Meiningen. This first professional position for a young composer lacking any significant conducting experience marked a major turning point in his life: until now Strauss was only a remarkable talent, a composer whose music was well crafted but hardly extraordinary. Away from friends and family and under the wing of Bülow and, ultimately, Alexander Ritter, Strauss would find his own voice and establish his own name as a composer and as a musician.

2 "Onward and away to ever-new victories": Strauss's emergence as a tone poet

The Meiningen assistantship to Hans von Bülow was a major opportunity for any aspiring conductor, and, not surprisingly, he received a flood of applications, a talented pool that included, among others, the 25-year-old Gustav Mahler. The heavy competition only makes the choice of Strauss, twenty-one years old and entirely inexperienced, all the more curious, especially since had he not formally applied for the position. Bülow had been building a strategy to bring the composer to Meiningen as early as May 1885, during that dark period of Josephine Strauss's first institutionalization. It was an obvious act of favoritism on the part of Bülow, but it was favoritism of the purest sort, one based on his instinctive feeling that this was a young man of enormous talent and immense potential. In Berlin Strauss had made a remarkable impression on Bülow, who believed him to be the "most original composer since Brahms," and it was an impression sustained in Munich by the premiere of Strauss's Suite Op. 4 and by the later premiere of his Horn Concerto Op. 5 in Meiningen. Bülow's decision to take Strauss on as a protégé, to become a kind of second paternal figure, had nothing to do with the influence of Richard's father, something Franz Strauss soon learned after he thanked Bülow for arranging the Munich premiere of his son's Op. 4: "You have nothing to thank me for," Bülow snapped (remembering his tirades against Wagner for the premieres of *Tristan* and *Meistersinger*), "I have not forgotten what you have done to me in this damned city of Munich.

What I did for your son was because he has talent and not for you."[1] A humbled Franz, for once, had no reply.

Strauss's period of study with Bülow, which began on 1 October 1885, was short, intense, and it profoundly affected the rest of his life as both conductor and composer. The young musician, who had never studied conducting, would learn by seeing and doing from one of Europe's finest practitioners. Beyond attending all rehearsals, with pencil and score in hand and occasionally the orchestral baton, Strauss was given full responsibility for the Choral Society, which consisted of some eighty women, to be augmented by men's chorus for certain concerts. Convinced that Strauss could master nearly any task put before him, Bülow took delight in putting the young man to the test. The well-noted premiere of Strauss's Suite in Munich (18 November 1884), when he gave the composer the baton to conduct (without rehearsal) for the first time in his life, was the first of many such tests. And the hectic first month in Meiningen offered another opportunity for the entirely inexperienced Strauss to prove himself.

During the first week of the month, Strauss dutifully attended orchestral rehearsals that included Beethoven Symphonies 1, 5, 6, and 7 (as well as the Egmont Overture and Fourth Piano Concerto), Brahms's two piano concerti, Tragic Overture, and Symphonies 1 and 3. Meanwhile Strauss began rehearsing Mozart's Requiem with the Choral Society and the next day played the K. 491 Piano Concerto in rehearsal using his own cadenzas. The next week was no less strenuous, and it saw Strauss conducting his first orchestral rehearsals: his new Symphony no. 2 in F minor, Brahms's Violin Concerto, and the A major Serenade. At the end of the second week, with Bülow out of town, members of the royal family decided to visit one of Strauss's rehearsals. Following custom, he asked his patrons whether they had a specific musical request, and Strauss was no doubt taken aback when Princess Marie, herself a fine pianist, asked for an extemporaneous reading of Wagner's *The Flying Dutchman* overture, which Strauss had never studied but nonetheless conducted with success. This impromptu event was the first Wagner that Strauss had ever conducted.

Week three saw the arrival of Johannes Brahms, who on his second day heard Strauss in concert as piano soloist (Mozart K. 491) and composer-conductor (the Symphony in F minor). Strauss visited Brahms regularly over the next few days, and it was during those visits that the elder composer offered advice that echoed his earlier judgment of the Suite, Op. 4: Strauss lacked cogent, well-shaped themes.

> Young man, take a close look at Schubert's dances and practice inventing simple eight-bar melodies . . . There's too much thematic trifling in your symphony; all that piling-up of a large number of themes [based] on a triad, with only rhythmic contrast between them, has no value whatever.[2]

Brahms had put his finger on a problem of which Strauss was undoubtedly aware, for his father had already been urging him toward thematic clarity and simplicity, and it is telling that Richard omitted Brahms's critique when he reported Brahms's visit to his father. But thanks to Ludwig Thuille who was also in Meiningen for the concert, Franz learned of it anyway, and he took full advantage of the situation:

> I was delighted to hear about the advice that Brahms gave you, about your use of counterpoint. My dear son, I ask that you take this honest and sincere advice to heart. – It has troubled me greatly that in all of your newer works you have paid more attention to contrapuntal effects than to natural, healthy invention and execution. Craftsmanship should never be noticeable. When it predominates it is only craft and no longer art. In art the truly magical and divine often lie in the subconscious. That is simply the way it is, no one can change it . . . one can achieve greatness only through clarity and simplicity![3]

Annoyed as he was that his father found out about Brahms's remarks, Strauss knew that he was right, that inspiration and technique – the spontaneous and the worked over – were too often out of balance (in favor of the latter) in his more recent orchestral works. Finding the proper balance was a lifelong struggle for Strauss who ultimately echoed his father's observations in a late essay from the 1940s. In it he,

4   Hans von Bülow: conductor, pianist, champion of Wagner and Brahms, and
    Strauss's great mentor

too, observes that great melody comes not from the intellect but from the unconscious, "uninfluenced by reason." Mozart's music would become the paradigm of great melody for Strauss, but that ultimate realization still eluded him, for now Strauss was in the midst of his "Brahmsschwärmerei," and he was also becoming increasingly drawn to Wagner.

In his memoirs Strauss credited his so-called "conversion" to Wagner and the music of the future to Alexander Ritter, an outspoken proponent of the ideals of Liszt and Wagner and thirty-one years Strauss's senior. Ritter had known both composers personally; his mother, Julie Ritter, was an ardent Wagner supporter and close friend. Alexander married Wagner's niece, Franziska, and he was a classmate and lifelong friend of Bülow, whom he followed to Meiningen, playing first violin in the orchestra. Ritter was also a composer of opera, lieder, and orchestral music, and Strauss became a perennial champion of his work. In his later years, Strauss looked back fondly to his meeting Ritter, which he called the "greatest event of the winter in Meiningen," an event during this brief period as Bülow's assistant that remains overemphasized in the Strauss literature. True, Ritter would become Strauss's third and final mentor, but the influence of Ritter was one that grew in intensity over a number of years, particularly after he left Meiningen. The Strauss–Ritter relationship was close, intense, and vital, though it remains problematic for several reasons: the host of undocumentable conversations and, of course, the lost correspondence. Strauss's retrospective on this important relationship, as valuable as it is, should hardly be taken at face value:

As a result of my upbringing, I still had some prejudices against Wagner's and especially Liszt's work, and I scarcely knew Richard Wagner's writings at all. Ritter, with patient explanations, introduced me to them and to Schopenhauer; he made me familiar with them and proved to me that the road led from the "musical expressionist" Beethoven ("Music as Expression" in Friedrich von Hausegger's phrase as against Hanslick's "Of Beauty in Music") via Liszt who, with Wagner, had realized correctly that Beethoven had

expanded the sonata form to its utmost limits . . . and that in
Beethoven's successors and especially Brahms, sonata form had
become an empty shell.[4]

But that is precisely what many biographers did, focusing on that
Meiningen winter as Strauss's "turning point" or moment of "conversion" to the music and aesthetics of Wagner and Liszt. In his senti-
mental reminiscence of the Meiningen period, Strauss collapsed
years of evolving thought into a single event. We know from the previous chapter that Strauss attended lectures on Schopenhauer during
his 1881 winter semester at the university, and he enthusiastically discussed the philosopher's writings with friends Arthur Seidl and
Friedrich Rösch. His so-called "prejudices against Wagner" had
already softened considerably by 1885, when – as letters home show –
he was rapidly asserting his musical independence. He had, indeed,
known all of Wagner's major works a few years before coming to
Meiningen, and clearly his "Brahmsschwärmerei" overlapped significantly with his increasing fascination with the aura of Bayreuth.

Still, the force of Ritter on the maturing Strauss should not be mini-
mized. His success in expanding Strauss's knowledge of Wagner's
and Hausegger's writings was the logical consequence of the young
composer's emerging personal style. In short, Ritter offered Strauss,
who was already conversant in Wagner's music, an aesthetic focus
and a means of achieving a level of inspiration that Brahms and Franz
Strauss said was lacking. And though Ritter did not introduce Strauss
to Schopenhauer, we shall see later that he offered a slant on *The World
as Will and Representation* that was highly idiosyncratic and would ultimately be rejected by Strauss. Ritter's most important, and least recognized, contribution to Strauss's development was the introduction
to the music of Franz Liszt, especially his symphonic poems. "Onkel
Ritter," as Strauss would call his avuncular friend, first met Liszt in the
1840s and began playing first violin in Liszt's Weimar Court Orchestra
in 1854, and the friendship continued until Liszt's death in 1886.
Strauss proclaimed the slogan "new ideas must seek new forms" to be
the "basic principle of Liszt's symphonic works," and he credited

Ritter for helping him realize this central tenet of the "music of the future."

And here we return to the Straussian enigma. Just what was Strauss absorbing during this important year? On one evening, such as 24 October, he would spend hours alone with Brahms, while on the next he would talk late into the night with Ritter, whose intense dislike for Brahms was known to all. But above all it was Bülow who served as an important model for bridging the gap between the "music of the future" and classic Romanticism. An ardent champion of Wagner in his younger years, he had long since tempered his admiration after Wagner had taken away his wife Cosima, daughter of Liszt, yet he maintained great respect for Wagner's music if not the man. However, Bülow maintained equal – if not greater – enthusiasm for Brahms in his later years, and this was the part of Bülow that rubbed off on young Strauss. Bülow left it to his old friend Ritter to proselytize on behalf of Bayreuth and its narrow orbit.

There was another aspect of Meiningen that would leave an indelible mark on Strauss, an experience connected neither to Ritter nor to Bülow, yet one that would profoundly shape Strauss's career many years later: that of the theater. The Meiningen Theater of the 1880s was one of the finest in Germany for its size, and Strauss the avid theatergoer took full advantage. Strauss certainly enjoyed the social company of some of the actresses, especially one Cäcilie Wenzel, much to his father's annoyance, but Richard's letters home suggest a strong attachment to the stage and a thorough knowledge of the dramatic repertoire. His diaries and letters document his exposure to Schiller, Kleist, Shakespeare, Ibsen, Lessing, Lindner, and others. Such an intense preoccupation with the theater would not resurface until he went to Berlin in 1898, and it was a major factor in his move from tone poem to opera.

Strauss was barely two months in Meiningen when Bülow put him to yet another test. It was well known that Bülow would not be staying in Meiningen much longer, but no one predicted that he would suddenly resign his post by the end of November, sadly the day after

Strauss's mother was institutionalized for a second time. The precise reason for the abrupt resignation remains unclear, and there was most likely a combination of factors. The proud, temperamental Bülow gave the baton to Brahms for the Meiningen premiere of his Fourth Symphony, and the composer was to reciprocate for the important Frankfurt premiere, but at the last minute Brahms took the podium, a move that incensed Bülow, who then resigned from Meiningen and went on an extended conducting tour in St. Petersburg leaving the 21-year-old Strauss in full charge of orchestra, chorus, and chamber concerts.

No sooner had Bülow given his farewell address than Karl von Perfall, Intendant of the Munich Hofkapelle, invited Strauss to become third conductor in his Vaterstadt. Bülow was skeptical: "You are one of those exceptional musicians who do not need to serve from the ranks upwards, who are of the caliber to take over one of the higher posts of command right away." He advised Strauss to wait until Levi retired as first conductor and then "step into his place without . . . going up the bureaucratic promotional ladder."[5] Strauss may well have seen handwriting on the wall that Bülow had earlier seen, for the Duke of Meiningen was planning to reduce musical activities severely, and without other offers Strauss had no choice but to go to Munich.

As busy as Strauss was during those final months in Meiningen he managed to compose his most important work to date: the *Burleske* for piano and orchestra. Begun in January, it was completed by April and, with Brahms in Meiningen for a visit, Strauss played through the mostly completed piece with the orchestra, though the premiere would not take place for another five years. The piano part betrays the strong influence of Brahms, especially the doublings and much of the figuration; his two piano concerti had clearly made their mark, and Strauss was quite open that this work represented the high point of his "Brahmsschwärmerei." But this remarkably modern piece, Strauss's first work of real independence, with its irreverent tongue-in-cheek qualities that foreshadow *Don Juan*, is one of the earliest pieces to use the historical canon as a source for parody. Perhaps it was his solution to the Brahms–Wagner quandary of 1886, and in a typically Straussian way, it is resolved through humor, for the composer takes clear delight in burlesquing Brahms (with the piano concerti) and Wagner. Especially humorous is the exaggerated prolongation of the *Tristan* chord in the cadenza and the references to the opening storm scene from *Die Walküre*, in the same D minor key as the *Burleske* itself. Though musical citation was a time-honored tradition in the nineteenth century, in the *Burleske*, with its irreverent citations, Strauss forges a new relationship between composer, performer, and audience, for without the audience's knowledge of works from recent history that fragile sense of parody would collapse. Woodwind pieces, symphonies, and a horn concerto were all tried-and-true genres where Strauss's amazing abilities showed through, and they earned the respect and admiration of his mentor, but the *Burleske* was another matter. For the first time Strauss, the fledgling modernist, had struck out on his own, and it was simply too much for Bülow, who deemed the work too busy and even unplayable, and the piece was ultimately premiered in 1890 by Eugène d'Albert whom Strauss had known since his first visit to Berlin.

Before taking up his Munich post on 1 August 1886, Strauss spent most of his spring touring Italy, a trip that was planned months ahead of time. We know much about his trip from letters home and from letters to Cäcilie Wenzel of the Meiningen Theater, his last link to his old post; their brief love affair would not survive his move to Munich. Strauss sought Italy not for its music but its landscape, architecture, and museums. In Bologna he heard *Aida* ("Indianermusik") and in Rome he heard *The Barber of Seville* ("it's such trash . . . can only be enjoyed in an outstanding performance"). But while he was in the Italian capital he met Franz von Lenbach, one of the most distinguished German painters of his day, and they spent regular evenings at the Roman taverns. In May he visited Naples, Sorrento, Salerno, Capri, and then returned to Rome. From there he wrote to his mother reporting on all the sites he had seen, also mentioning that he had begun composing. In the left-hand margin of the letter he annotated tonalities by each of the described Italian sites: C major, A major, G major, and C minor. The marginalia no doubt saw their way into *Aus Italien* (1886), which consists of movements in G major, C major, A major, and G major, respectively.

Back in Munich Strauss began systematic work on his tonal impressions, which would be a four-movement work that he described as a "first step toward independence." *Aus Italien* would be Strauss's first assay into the realm of the extra-musical, and – as he confessed to Bülow – he had "never really believed in inspiration through the beauty of nature, but in the Roman ruins I learned better, for ideas just came flying to me."[6] *Aus Italien* was the only work where the composer himself published a specific program: The first movement ("Auf der Campagna": *andante*) comes the closest to Liszt in construction and is based on three themes. The second ("Im Roms Ruinen": *allegro con brio*) suggests "fantastic images of vanished glory" and betrays the clearest affinity to Brahms in structure, phraseology, and scoring. The third movement ("Am Strande von Sorrent": *andantino*) represents his first serious attempt at musical pictorialism and serves as an early example of Strauss's unique ability to conjure up vivid sonic pictures primarily through orchestrational craft. Most controversial was the fourth movement ("Neapolisches Volksleben": *allegro*), which Strauss claimed to be based on "a well-known Neapolitan folk song, and in addition a tarantella [he] had heard in Sorrento." Of course, the venerable folk song was nothing more than the popular "Funiculi, funicula" composed by Luigi Danza in 1880 to celebrate the construction of the funicular on Mount Vesuvius, which Strauss had visited, in its active phase, while in Italy. Strauss was on the mark when he described it as a "hilarious jumble of themes," for it is surely an amusing hodgepodge where, in the development, motives generated from "Funiculi, funicula" interact in a setting more appropriate to *Elektra*.

While Strauss was at work on *Aus Italien*, King Ludwig II and his physician (the very physician who had treated Strauss's mother in Eglfing) died mysteriously on 12 June 1886, an event that would indirectly affect Strauss in his new position, given that the Royal Opera House would no longer enjoy Ludwig's unprecedented level of support. In early August Strauss traveled with Ritter to Bayreuth both to visit the grave of the recently deceased Franz Liszt and to hear *Tristan* and *Parsifal*; thereafter Strauss was ready to take up his Munich duties, though he would face some harsh realities. At age twenty-two, Strauss was talented and brash: two traits that annoyed his superiors and complicated his life considerably during the three years he served in Munich. On paper, the Munich post (though as third conductor) was a better position, and he was able to return to a richer cultural center as well. But in Meiningen he operated with remarkable autonomy, admired by his patrons and by Bülow, while Munich required him to fit into a more rigid, bureaucratic hierarchy that often seemed to reward seniority over talent. Worse yet, Hermann Levi, first conductor at the Court Opera, was often ill, which put in charge the detested second conductor, Franz Fischer ("a criminal at the rostrum," according to Strauss). Still worse, the Intendant, Karl von Perfall – himself a conductor and composer of sorts – was both hostile to Strauss's music and to his "Bülowian" style of conducting. Strauss readily admitted that because he insisted on his own tempi, taking the baton at short notice made it difficult for singers and musicians, who included his father on first horn. Strauss was unhappy, and he made many of those around him equally so, including Levi himself. Franz Strauss advised patience and moderation to his often hot-headed son, who was bored with a second-string repertoire that included Boieldieu, Auber, and Donizetti.

If there was any solace to Strauss's new arrangement in Munich, it was the fact that his friend Ritter had also left Meiningen for the Bavarian capital. Moreover, old friends and schoolmates such as Ludwig Thuille and Friedrich Rösch were also in town. Strauss may have had higher pay but he had ultimately less to do than in Meiningen and, less preoccupied with conducting duties, he spent more time composing and thinking about philosophy and musical aesthetics, and his relationship with Ritter deepened considerably.

Their friendship was complex, and one should not infer that the excitable, often overbearing Ritter exerted absolute influence. His idiosyncratic fusion of Catholicism, Schopenhauer, Liszt, and Wagner was surely at odds with the agnostic Strauss, who ultimately found Ritter's religio-mystical views on the ethical properties of music difficult to accept. But they remained friends throughout the 1880s, the elder Ritter continuing to stimulate Strauss's thoughts on music and philosophy (mostly Schopenhauer), which in 1887 found their way into the early stages of a libretto he was writing for his first opera, *Guntram*, which was not completed until 1893.

The site for these numerous discussions was the Weinstube Leibenfrost, where Onkel Ritter, Strauss, Rösch, and Thuille would gather nearly every evening at six with Ritter always at the head of the table; occasionally Franz Strauss would attend as well. These meetings were critical to Strauss's development, for though he was aware of the epistemological foundation of Schopenhauer's philosophy and of the mechanics of the Wagnerian musical apparatus, he had not made a connection between the two. Wagner was far more than mere style and technique, according to Ritter; his musical language was the vehicle for realizing the central tenet of Schopenhauerian metaphysics: the denial of the Will. We return, once again, to this tension in Strauss's life between expression and technique, between subject and object: in short, between content and form. And though we have no documentation for those meetings, Strauss's letter to Bülow in August 1888 suggests how his musical thought had evolved since his days in Meiningen:

> From the F minor symphony onwards I have found myself in a gradually ever-increasing contradiction between the musical-poetic content that I want to convey and the ternary sonata form that has come down to us from the classical composers. In the case of Beethoven the musical-poetic content was for the most part completely covered by the very "*Sonata form*," which he raised to its highest point, wholly expressing in it what he felt and wanted to say ... [but] what was for Beethoven a "form" absolutely in congruity

with the highest, most glorious content, is now, after 60 years, used as a formula inseparable from our instrumental music (which I strongly dispute), simply to accommodate and enclose a "pure musical" (in the strictest and narrowest meaning of the word) content, or worse, to stuff and expand a content with which it does not correspond. . . . I consider it a legitimate artistic method to create a correspondingly new form for every new subject, to shape which neatly and perfectly is a very difficult task, but for that very reason the more attractive.[7]

The genre of symphony was moribund, according to Strauss, it had become little more than arbitrary, random patterns: "giant's clothes made to fit a Hercules, in which a thin tailor is trying to comport himself elegantly." Convinced of an artist's duty to create a "new form for every new subject," Strauss tried to resolve this problem in *Macbeth*, for if *Aus Italien* had been a "first step" toward program music, *Macbeth* (though it did not premiere until after *Don Juan* and *Death and Transfiguration*) would be his first full-fledged tone poem, a work "that set out upon a completely new path."

But the path was not without detours, for *Macbeth* went through more changes and revisions than any of his other tone poems. Sketches compellingly demonstrate just how extensive the revisions actually were, especially in the development and recapitulation, and reveal a composer grappling seriously with the conflicting demands of narrative and structural paradigm. Those ill-fitting "giant's clothes" were not all that easy to cast off. Indeed, as Strauss got to the beginning of the development section, he stopped composing altogether and turned to a new piece, the Violin Sonata in E♭, which would be his final work using classic structural models until his so-called "Indian Summer" period of the 1940s. "Completely new path" or no, *Macbeth*, which had to wait two years for its premiere, failed to find a firm place in the concert repertoire. True, it had to compete with *Don Juan* and *Death and Transfiguration*, both of which achieved quick fame, but *Macbeth* lacked the cogency and convincing pacing of musical events so evident in the two subsequent works. And despite the revisions, where Strauss sought to restrain some of the inner voices in order to highlight better the principle themes, *Macbeth* still fell short of the other tone poems in sonic clarity and there was still too much of the "thematic trifling" that had so troubled Brahms after he had heard Strauss's Second Symphony.

Macbeth launched Strauss's journey into a new symphonic direction, that of the *Tondichtung* or tone poem (to be distinguished from Liszt's term "symphonic poem"), and this new project was one inextricably connected to those evening meetings at Leibenfrost's Weinstube. It was a journey of seven tone poems composed over a decade that can be subdivided into two periods of intense activity: the first "cycle" of tone poems (*Macbeth, Don Juan,* and *Death and Transfiguration*) was composed during the years 1887–89; the second cycle (*Till Eulenspiegel, Also sprach Zarathustra, Don Quixote,* and *Ein Heldenleben*) – begun after Strauss's preoccupation with his first opera, *Guntram* – was composed between 1895 and 1898. Strauss left no doubt as to the importance of his Leibenfrost friends in the creation of these new works: *Macbeth* was dedicated to Ritter, *Don Juan* to Thuille, and *Death and Transfiguration* to Rösch. These three men were the closest friends that Strauss would ever have in his life. Much has been made of Strauss's friendship with Ritter and Thuille, but the bond between Strauss and Rösch was no less strong. Their friendship dated back to the Gymnasium days; Rösch was two years ahead, and though he was also a fairly accomplished musician, he ultimately became an attorney and worked in the area of copyright law with Strauss in later years. A visibly shaken Strauss paid tribute to his friend at a funeral service in 1925: "I have always owed recreation, inspiration and stimulation to his unshakable loyalty, his all-embracing knowledge, his insuperable idealism and his truly productive and acute criticism." A disciple of Ritter, Rösch married his daughter Marie, and he shared his father-in-law's enthusiasm for Schopenhauer, maintaining a firm belief in the transcendent, ethical properties of music.

One would look in vain for anything ethical or sacred in the tone poem *Don Juan*, a work described by Carl Dahlhaus as the "dawning of

5 Strauss in 1888, shortly after leaving Munich for Weimar

'musical modernism.'" It is difficult, indeed, to fathom that only months after *Macbeth* Strauss could have composed a work so far advanced beyond anything he had yet written. *Don Juan's* provocative subject matter, its brilliant orchestration, its highly profiled, often evocative themes, and its sure-footed, concise pacing of musical events created a sensation at the time and earned Strauss his stature as the leading symphonic composer of his day. If Strauss earlier had found himself trapped in an escalating antithesis between poetic content and formal structure, *Don Juan* represents a bold, convincing solution where Strauss created a novel musical structure at one with its programmatic material, where narrative and formal strategies did not seem forced upon each other. Is the work in some sort of rondo form? Or in a modified sonata structure? Or, perhaps, some sort of synthesis of the two? The work, and nearly all the tone poems thereafter, have brought with them a host of challenges for musical analysts.

In finding a garment that finally fit its subject, Strauss also had found his voice as a tone poet, but in doing so he appeared to be distancing himself from the redemptive, spiritual concerns voiced by Ritter and Rösch. The Don always races "toward new victories," but they are triumphs of the bedroom, not the battlefield. *Don Juan* is flagrantly pictorial, funny, and altogether secular, with a "hero" who enjoys thumbing his nose at the world. If there is something of the philosophical essence of Leibenfrost in *Don Juan*, it is in its progressive, anti-Philistine (read anti-Munich) spirit. Without any documentation, we can only wonder what Ritter's deeper thoughts about the work must have been. Did he already detect the seeds of that part of Strauss he would come to reject by 1893, namely that in Act III of *Guntram*: "nothing of Wagner's world view remains in you [only] the mechanics of his art." Certainly in *Don Juan* we see a composer immersed in Wagner's musical style and technique though far removed from his artistic philosophy. In *Don Juan* we see a composer using Wagner's "sacred apparatus" (as Ritter would have seen it), his "sacred language" to demythologize the philosophy that gave us that very language.

The unprecedented power and cogency of Don Juan may well have been catalyzed by someone entirely unrelated to the Leibenfrost circle, namely Strauss's private vocal student and future wife, Pauline de Ahna. They first became acquainted in August 1887 while vacationing at Lake Starnberg, and though she had at first enrolled in the vocal program at the Müncher Musikschule (later, the Akademie der Tonkunst), she soon became Strauss's private pupil for vocal coaching, and he had arranged for her to take acting lessons from Ritter's wife Franziska. Dora Wihan and Cäcilie Wenzel were old flames by now; Pauline, the proud, outspoken daughter of Major-General Adolf de Ahna, soon became more than a professional interest for Strauss, and it is hardly far-fetched to imagine that the libidinal fire of Don Juan was ignited by his future "Heldensgefährtin." Professional and personal interests overlapped significantly later in Weimar, where Strauss was to delight in coaching Pauline on a regular basis, though they remained per Sie. For Strauss's name day in April 1890 she made him an elaborate cake, and that following Christmas Strauss gave her a generous present.

True or not, Pauline was definitely the catalyst for another great part of the nineteenth-century Straussian repertoire, namely that of lieder. While in Meiningen Strauss already had composed his famed Op. 10 lieder, songs of unprecedented maturity (such as "Zueignung" and "Allerseelen") that continue to be mainstays of the repertoire. From that time until 1891, when he became preoccupied with completing Guntram, Strauss would produce a lieder opus (Opp. 15, 17, 19, 21, 22) every year. These were songs by lesser-known poets (Herrmann von Gilm, Adolf Friedrich von Schack, and Felix Dahn), for what Strauss required for composing lieder was not poems of high literary quality but texts with striking expressive images or situations that could ignite his imagination. Once Strauss had met Pauline – even seven years before their marriage – hers was the voice in his sonic imagination when he composed lieder.

The same summer that he met Pauline, he made the acquaintance of another woman who would play an important role in his career:

6 Friedrich Rösch, lifelong friend of the composer, attorney, and collaborator in
the establishment of rights for composers

Cosima Wagner, former wife of Bülow, widow of Wagner, and self-appointed custodian of the Bayreuth legacy. Despite pretensions to the contrary, Cosima was decidedly unphilosophical and thus complemented Ritter uniquely with her preoccupation with practical matters of Wagner performance. She was a tenacious widow who, when the great dispute heated up between Munich and Bayreuth over the ownership of Wagner's legacy (excluding Parsifal), was able to prevail in this battle of wills. Third conductor Strauss, who was not allowed to conduct the major Wagnerian works in Munich, increasingly enjoyed guest conducting (Berlin, Dresden, and Leipzig, where he first met Mahler) and was drawn ever closer to Bayreuth. It was a time when the future of the Festival was not altogether certain: Wagner, its guiding force, had died in 1883, and its chief sponsor, King Ludwig II, died three years later; few people believed that a woman who lacked business and musical training would be able to resurrect a festival that many critics believed to be nothing more than a passing fancy anyway. Strauss's early loyalty to Cosima was important and it ultimately paid big dividends.

Strauss was growing increasingly weary of the steady diet of Auber, Cornelius, and Nicolai and therefore greeted early confidential offers from the Weimar Court Opera with unguarded enthusiasm. In March 1889, a formal offer was made, and Strauss accepted the appointment of Kapellmeister (not Hofkapellmeister, as he had wanted) to the Grand Duke of Saxe-Weimar-Eisenach. The Weimar Intendant, Hans von Bronsart, had great respect for Bülow and had taken his enthusiastic recommendation to heart; the Music Director, Eduard Lassen, had likewise heard great things about Strauss. The wisdom of their decision was given further credibility when, shortly after his arrival, Cosima Wagner asked Strauss to work as music assistant that summer in Bayreuth. There he developed and maintained a close relationship with Wagner's widow, giving him notoriety and assuring Cosima of an ardent Wagner advocate in Weimar. The opera at Weimar, with its modest means, could never threaten Bayreuth, but with an enthusiastic "neo-Bayreuthian" such as Strauss, it could diminish the reputation of rival Munich and serve as a kind of regular-season promotional for the summer festival.

Strauss brought potential prestige to Weimar, with a portfolio that included the newly completed score to *Don Juan*, a nearly finished *Death and Transfiguration*, and early libretto sketches for his first opera, *Guntram*. He also brought with him his favorite singer from Munich, Pauline de Ahna. But before beginning his Weimar duties in 1889, there was a summer of Wagner ahead of him in Bayreuth, where he coached and rehearsed every morning. The works that summer included *Tristan* (under Felix Mottl), *Meistersinger* (under Hans Richter), and *Parsifal* (under Hermann Levi). An enthusiastic Strauss quite rightly saw this as a first step that would ultimately lead to conducting one of his own productions, perhaps with his favorite soprano in a lead role. Indeed, Pauline visited the festival for a week in August and was presumably introduced to Cosima. Also in town for much of the festival were Strauss's Leibenfrost cohorts Ritter, Rösch, and Thuille.

With greater responsibilities, and a sense of autonomy reminiscent of those Meiningen days, Strauss threw himself into his new tasks with unprecedented energy. Thanks to his bad experience in Munich, he learned much about the bureaucratic and political realities of running a large opera company, and he was surely not going to repeat earlier mistakes. Strauss's conducting mission in Weimar was double-pronged: he wanted on the one hand to make it an important center for "authentic" Wagner performance, and on the other to honor Franz Liszt, his legendary Weimar predecessor, through championing his symphonic poems. And Strauss remained a loyal advocate of the music (especially the two operas) of his friend, Ritter, though it was not a primary focus. Active in the opera pit as well as on the symphony podium, he was also making great progress as a composer. *Don Juan* premiered early on in Weimar to great acclaim.

The substantial correspondence between Strauss and Cosima Wagner during this period reveals a complex relationship where idealism and self-promotion intertwined with one another in unique ways. Genuinely inspired by his experience in Bayreuth, Strauss – with altruistic zeal – wanted to replicate that very tradition in Weimar, but he also saw in Cosima an advocate who could help further his career in the short term (perhaps a Bayreuth conducting invitation) and in the long term (a possible conducting post at a more prestigious opera house). Likewise, Cosima was delighted that someone wished to conduct her late-husband's works with the utmost care, but she also saw a potential ally in her musical-political war with Munich. And the fact that the son of her husband's mortal enemy, Franz Strauss, had been won over to the Bayreuth camp was not at all lost on Cosima, who was not only eager to bring Strauss into the Bayreuth circle but also into the Wagner family. Her designs included Strauss possibly marrying her daughter Eva, and, of course, she encouraged the friendship between Strauss and her son, Siegfried, who – with the help of his family name – enjoyed a modest career as a composer and conductor. The protective Cosima was proud of her son's accomplishments and believed that a relationship with the talented Strauss could only help his career.

Even those familiar with Strauss's prodigious capacity for work were amazed by the energy with which he programmed, rehearsed, conducted, and composed while in Weimar. His programming for the opening fall orchestral season included an ambitious list of *Zukunftsmusik* that, according to Strauss himself, caused Bronsart to "throw up his hands": Berlioz's *Symphonie fantastique*; Bülow's *Nirvana*; Liszt's *Ideale*, *Festklänge*, and *Orpheus*; songs by Ritter; and Wagner's *Faust* Overture and *Siegfried Idyll*. Still, Bronsart and Lassen were eager to keep their new young talent, and for the most part yielded to Strauss's plans. Wishing to prove himself worthy of Cosima's trust, Strauss decided that his first major operatic project in Weimar should be a production of *Lohengrin*, which had, after all, received its world premiere under Liszt in Weimar in 1850 and was approaching its hundredth performance. The hours spent coaching and rehearsing were without precedent in the city. During the previous August in Bayreuth, Strauss had discussed his plans thoroughly

7 Franz Liszt, one of Strauss's spiritual mentors, and his daughter Cosima with
   whom Strauss developed an important artistic bond in the late 1880s and early
   1890s

with Cosima, who offered general advice with regard to tempi and
quite specific suggestions involving style of singing, enunciation, and
stage directions. After the premiere Strauss wrote her a lengthy letter
detailing all aspects of the performance, to which she replied: "You
have described everything with such vivid precision that I feel as if I
were experiencing your production of *Lohengrin* myself."[8]

Cosima did ultimately witness a Weimar performance of *Lohengrin*
in February 1890, accompanied by her daughter, Eva. Despite a small

orchestra and the necessity of two small cuts, the production received enthusiastic reviews and received the strong approval of Cosima herself. While she was in Weimar Strauss, in his youthful zeal, performed his new Don Juan for her on the piano, and Cosima was, frankly, disappointed: "It seemed to me, in your Don Juan, that you were more interested in the presentation of your characters than in the way your characters had spoken to you. I call that the play of intelligence against emotions."[9] Her comment resembles Ritter's later criticism that Strauss had abandoned Wagner's philosophy and had retained only "the mechanics of his art," for Cosima, the guardian of her late husband's ideals, was offended not only by the blatantly erotic subject matter but by the concreteness of his musical narrative. She urged him to follow his heart and not become preoccupied with surface elements that delight only the brain. Taking her cue from Wagner's "On Franz Liszt's Symphonic Poems (1857)," she suggested that rather than create evocative themes Strauss should seek "eternal motives" that can be perceived and understood at various levels and in various manifestations. Strauss's reply was polite, even deferential: "I think I have understood [you] correctly and I look forward to producing evidence next time we meet, in the form of my third symphonic work [Tod und Verklärung] . . . that I have perhaps already made a significant advance, even in the choice of subject."[10] The subject of his next work, Tod und Verklärung, is, indeed, more elevated, but it is doubtful that Cosima's advice affected his personal artistic views in any serious way.

Yet, unlike Don Juan, it bears a far more recognizable stamp of Ritter who wrote a post-compositional poetic preface published with the score. This poem, which speaks of "world-redemption" and "world-transfiguration," is saturated with the transcendent flavor of late Wagner (one thinks of Tristan and Parsifal). It has also been criticized by some as being too detailed and largely extraneous to Strauss's expressive aims, but Ritter's influence on Strauss during this critical time was more important than many commentators have realized. Though the work is pure Strauss, who resisted Ritter's suggested subtitle ("Seraphic Fantasy," after Goethe), this tone poem comes the closest of all to Ritter's ideals of music, redemption, and transcendence.

Tod und Verklärung, the most metaphysical of his tone poems, is based not on a pre-existent literary text (as were the two previous symphonic works) but rather on a narrative of the composer's own conception: a dying artist, obsessed by an artistic Ideal, is transfigured at death to recognize his Ideal in eternity. The noble melody for the Ideal itself may well have been inspired by a theme from Ritter's symphonic dance Olafs Hochzeitsreigen, which Strauss had recommended (June 1890) to Alfred Sieger (Director of the Frankfurt Museum Concerts) for possible programming. In Tod und Verklärung death is less the issue than transfiguration: with its abundant musical possibilities, it had a life-long fascination for Strauss that manifests itself in various ways from Rosenkavalier through the Metamorphosen. Indeed, typical of Strauss, there is a specifically musical allegory for this concept in the tone poem, where the theme of the Ideal goes through various transformations.

Despite the loftier subject matter, the work contains modernistic touches of musical realism that likely irritated Cosima Wagner, though she claimed to be gripped by the work, especially by its conciseness and unity of expression. The tone poem is cast in a modified sonata form which begins with a quiet, syncopated introduction ("breathing irregularly"), then an agitated exposition ("racked by terrible pain"), followed by an episodic developmental space: dreams of childhood, youthful passions. What follows is the principal theme of the work – that of the artistic Ideal, which goes through various musical transfigurations. The restatement of this lofty melody in the extended coda (what Strauss called the "point of culmination") is one of the most exquisite moments of all his symphonic works. Even Strauss's father, Franz, remarked that this close created a deeply "moving effect that no one could otherwise imagine." It was indeed Strauss's most profound work to date and, despite the touches of pictorialism (irregular heart beats, the use of tam-tam when the soul leaves the body), Tod und Verklärung stands apart from all the other tone poems in the way it sustains a consistent elevated, serious mode of expression. (The only other orchestral work to do so is the *Metamorphosen* of 1944.) In this final work that thoroughly bears the mark of his mentor, Alexander Ritter, we see Strauss's view of a divinity rooted in humanity's ideas and deeds. Through inspiration and striving, the protagonist is able to rise above normal life, not unlike the protagonist of Strauss's *Wandrers Sturmlied* (1885) who hovers above the earth, *göttergleich* (like the gods).

The reception of *Tod und Verklärung* in June 1890 was overwhelmingly positive; Strauss had finally achieved the reputation of the greatest tone poet of his day, and he was able to sell the work to his old friend and publisher Eugen Spitzweg for 1600 Marks (twice the amount for *Don Juan*) as well as stipulate that he should publish his unsuccessful *Macbeth*. After the Vienna premiere even the predictably skeptical critic Eduard Hanslick had to admit the work's brilliance of execution and went so far as to declare that *Tod und Verklärung* "exemplifies a composer moving in the direction of music drama." Hanslick was, of course, unaware that Strauss was already in the midst of composing his first opera, *Guntram*, for *Tod und Verklärung* ends the feverish tone poem activity of the 1880s, a time when Ritter's influence was at its strongest. In this three-act work, Guntram (a Tannhäuser-like minnesinger) flouts the rules of his pacifist Christian brotherhood when he kills the wicked Duke Robert (husband of the beloved Freihild) in a duel. This ethical fraternity, which saw art and music as a transcendent, redemptive space, sought to redeem Guntram from his transgression, though they ultimately failed. In the Wagnerian tradition, the libretto, finished in its first draft on 25 September 1890, was the product of the composer himself and, in its initial stages, would be informed strongly by his readings of Schopenhauer and Wagner, as well as his discussions with Ritter and Friedrich Rösch. Ritter, who had already composed some operas of his own, pinned great hope on Strauss's project, anticipating that it would contain the very aspects of "world redemption" that he believed to be contained in *Tod und Verklärung*.

It is hard to believe that Strauss could find much time to work on his first opera as busy as he was in Weimar conducting new productions of *Tannhäuser* and *Rienzi*, as well as the standard repertory operas of Mozart, Cornelius, and Lortzing, and a revised version of Gluck's *Iphigenia in Tauris*. Moreover, as his fame increased more and more invitations for guest conducting poured in: from Berlin, Cologne, Leipzig, and Frankfurt. He even received an invitation to conduct the New York Symphony Concerts for two years, an offer he reluctantly refused given the 30,000-Mark price tag. Added to all this was the crowning glory of his Weimar period: a new, and uncut, production of *Tristan* in 1892. Strauss was to have conducted *Tannhäuser* in Bayreuth (with Pauline as second Elisabeth) during the summer of 1891, but a serious bout of pneumonia that spring postponed those plans for a couple of years. During that period of convalescence he studied the *Tristan* score with great intensity. Rehearsals that autumn took place with an intensity that surpassed those for the earlier *Lohengrin* production. Strauss spoke of "gigantic *Arrangierenproben*" to Cosima, adding that "Weimar has never seen the like before and the whole town is talking about them." He later remarked to her that the premiere (17 January 1892) represented "the happiest day of my life."

All of this happy, feverish activity as conductor and composer (he had begun the *Guntram* Act I prelude in March) left Strauss completely exhausted, and by the end of the 1891–92 season he had become gravely ill with pleurisy. Bayreuth was again out of the question as he convalesced during the summer, composing *Guntram* in bed, and he took a leave from Weimar spending the winter in the warmer climates of Greece and Egypt. The resilient Strauss turned this period of recuperation into a kind of *Bildungsreise*, for it was during this time of solitary journey that he intensified his study of philosophy and aesthetics. It was a critical turning point in his career, for the distance from Ritter allowed Strauss to work out important differences he had with his avuncular friend. His travel diaries, full of philosophical commentaries, detail not only an immersion in the writings of Wagner, Plato, and Sophocles but a preoccupation with Schopenhauer, Nietzsche, and probably Max Stirner. These readings inspired other potential operatic projects as well: a *Don Juan* opera, *Das erhabene Lied der Könige*, *Der Reichstag zu Mainz*, and an opera to be based on the Till Eulenspiegel legend. None of these projects ever got beyond libretto sketches.

By the time Strauss left for Greece (6 November 1892) he had already finished composing Acts I and II of *Guntram*. By Act III, which hinges upon the issue of redemption and atonement, he had reached a moment of impasse, for after some more careful rereading of Schopenhauer's *World as Will and Representation*, especially the fourth and final book, he realized that his view of the denial of the Will and Ritter's could never be reconciled, and, indeed, he was moving beyond Schopenhauer altogether. This revised final act, where Guntram seeks redemption by abandoning his fraternal order and his art, can be read as an abandonment of Wagnerian metaphysics – at least that is how a horrified Alexander Ritter interpreted it, and as a result, his intense friendship with Strauss was seriously damaged. The contrast with a work such as *Tannhäuser* is instructive, for where Tannhäuser travels to Rome for penance, Guntram – who was originally going to make a pilgrimage to the Holy Land – sets off on his own solitary path, leaving behind his fraternal order and his beloved Freihild. In short, Guntram "abandoned art for the sake of spiritual redemption" (Strauss, paradoxically, taking Schopenhauer, especially Book 4 of his *The World as Will and Representation*, far more seriously than most of his contemporaries) and, of course, Strauss covertly bade farewell to metaphysics, especially Ritter's idiosyncratic brand of Wagnerism.[11] Ritter implored his "protégé" to rethink the ending, but Strauss refused, and by the following September the entire opera was finished. After extensive and ultimately futile negotiations with Munich, a premiere was slated for May 1894 in Weimar.

Schopenhauer had become the philosophical gospel for many German composers of Strauss's generation. What fascinated them was the philosopher's elevation of music above all other arts as a non-representational "thing-in-itself." For if painting and literature represented the phenomenal, music – so powerful, yet invisible – was the noumenal, a representation of the Will itself. But life, according to Schopenhauer, was a realm of suffering; desire and longing would always exceed their fulfillment. Thus, the Will was ultimately a negative force, one that should be suppressed, even better, denied. Book 3 of *The World as Will and Representation* claims that through art, music being the highest form, the individual can become "a pure, Will-less subject of knowledge," thus supressing the Will. Most non-academic discussions of Schopenhauer among this generation of composers dwelt upon this important third book, but Strauss's experience with Schopenhauer dated back to 1881, and in the early 1890s, especially during his solitary trip to Greece and Egypt, he returned to Schopenhauer with renewed enthusiasm, and he explored the fourth and final book, which seems to turn an about-face on art, which can only suppress but never entirely deny the Will. Strauss's annotations in his copy of the book suggest his lack of sympathy with a philosophy that squarely placed religious asceticism or saintliness ahead of music as the only hope for permanent release from the Will, and the endless striving that it causes. In a typically self-deprecating way, Strauss made light of his rejection of Schopenhauerian saintliness in a letter to Cosima: "I can't help it, I'll never be granted the halo." Strauss's readings of Stirner and, especially, Nietzsche would help him through this time of crisis; and they would be made manifest in such works as *Also sprach Zarathustra*.

The year 1894 saw a cascade of events that would profoundly affect Strauss's life, for not only was his friendship with Ritter (the third and last paternal figure) irreparably damaged, Strauss lost his second father-figure, Hans von Bülow, on 12 February, although because of Strauss's intense artistic relationship with Bülow's ex-wife, Cosima, their friendship had cooled off somewhat. The circumstances surrounding the memorial concert for Bülow, who was buried in Hamburg, suggest the complexities of Bülow's late musical tastes and also how far from Bülow's influence Strauss had moved. When asked to form a concert (already scheduled for 26 February) for a Bülow memorial, Strauss eagerly suggested works by Beethoven,

Liszt, Wagner, and Bülow himself. The committee was incensed that no Brahms was programmed, and they felt that programming Wagner, who after all had taken Bülow's wife, was in poor taste. Strauss refused to accede to their demands and organized his own memorial in Leipzig a few days before the Hamburg tribute, which included a moving performance of the *Eroica* under Mahler.

But Bülow's death, the Ritter problem, and the coming *Guntram* premiere were among a host of significant events that took place in 1894. Shortly before the new year (Christmas Eve 1893) Strauss premiered Humperdink's *Hänsel und Gretel*, and his future wife was scheduled to introduce the role of Hänsel; a sprained ankle during rehearsal prevented Pauline's appearance. Though she was able to take over some performances a month later, a far greater artistic success for the young soprano was singing Elisabeth in Bayreuth (summer 1894), and under the baton of her fiancé, Richard Strauss, who had publicly announced their engagement on the day of *Guntram*'s 10 May premiere; Pauline sang the role of Freihild. Life seemed to be going Strauss's way: he finally was able to conduct in Bayreuth, he was happily engaged, he helped with musical preparations for the Allgemeiner deutscher Musikverein congress in Weimar (which included initial rehearsals for Mahler's First Symphony) and – after some extremely complex negotiations – he was appointed as Kapellmeister at the Munich Court Opera. But after a nine-year gap, Richard's mother was once again institutionalized for severe depression in Eglfing, and she had to miss the *Guntram* premiere, though she was able to attend her son's wedding on 10 September. After a honeymoon in Italy, Strauss was prepared to assume his Munich duties.

Strauss was not entirely delighted with the prospect of returning to Munich, in spite of the elevated position. Notwithstanding early positive assurances, negotiations got bogged down, for despite Generalmusikdirektor Hermann Levi's enthusiasm, neither Possart (Intendant of the Court Theater) nor Perfall (Intendant of the Court Opera) were entirely sure that Strauss should be the first choice.

Strauss was the most brilliant musician of his day, but he had developed a reputation for being difficult and demanding. Possart and Perfall held out hopes that Felix Mottl might accept their offer, and despite a written agreement in June 1893, Strauss was put on hold pending a last-minute agreement with Mottl, which fell through. Strauss saw through their duplicity and remained distrustful of the Munich management throughout his tenure in the Bavarian capital. He had neither forgotten his experience as third conductor in Munich, nor would he ever forgive the way his father was abruptly retired from his position in the orchestra in June 1889. And, of course, despite agreeing that he could conduct all the major Wagner operas, the Court Opera ultimately refused to offer the world premiere of *Guntram*. The May 1894 launching in Weimar met with lukewarm reviews and the later Munich Court Opera premiere (16 November 1895) was an outright failure. Future performances of *Guntram* were canceled, despite initial promises to the contrary, and for the first time Strauss had to deal, head on, with strong conservative elements in Munich. In short, Strauss's second tenure in Munich was poisoned from the start.

The failure of *Guntram* was the bitterest and most important setback of his life, at a time when Strauss was riding so high before the fall. He never forgot it, not even in the final weeks of his life, when in a short essay he lamented that most people had not recognized what was modern in his operas, a modernity that began with Act III of *Guntram*, where Strauss recognizes an unbreachable gap between the individual (Guntram) and the collective (Guntram's fraternal order). In Nietzschean terms this breach would be the "human" vs. the "metaphysical," and later, for Adorno, the gap between "subject" and "object." But Strauss, in a typically honest self-appraisal, assumed most of blame for *Guntram*'s failure himself. Indeed, he put up a grave marker in his back yard that read:

Here lies the venerable, virtuous young Guntram –
Minnesinger, who was gruesomely slain by the symphony orchestra
    of his own father.
May he rest in peace!

Though he never forgave Munich, he well knew that he had much to learn about composing opera, and here we see a parallel to the failure of *Macbeth*, his unsuccessful first venture into the genre of tone poem. From this latest setback Strauss recognized that he was no librettist, saw the dangers of stepping too near the Wagnerian shadow (even though by the end of the opera he was distancing himself from Bayreuth), realized the harshness of Munich's Philistinism, and, consciously or not, discovered that he needed to explore further the problem of narrative in a purely symphonic medium.

His move to Munich matched the earlier move from Meiningen to the Bavarian capital; in both cases he went from an experience of relative autonomy to one where a more complex musical hierarchy prevailed. But this time the thirty-year-old Strauss had far greater clout, and though he had to deal constantly with Levi, the detested Perfall, and Ernst von Possart, he usually got his way and very likely made life uncomfortable for these older men. Strauss and his wife had settled into their new quarters (Hildegardstrasse), and the regular nights out with the Leibenfrost cohorts had diminished considerably. Indeed, the old *Tafelrund*, with Ritter still at the head of the table, had grown considerably and moved to the Weinhaus Neuner, where it met once a week, Thursdays from 6 to 8 p.m. It was a much more formal and social affair and now included (beyond the nucleus of Ritter, Strauss, Thuille, and Rösch) Hermann Levi, Oskar Gura, Heinrich Poges, Arthur Seidl, Friedrich Klose, Ferdinand Löwe, Herman Zumpe, Max von Schillings, and even sometimes d'Albert or Busoni, if they were in town.

Strauss was delighted to be closer with his old childhood friend Thuille, who was now teaching piano and harmony at the Königliche Musikschule, and he also developed a closer relationship with Schillings. In both cases, Strauss diligently championed their various works with moderate success. But there was another composer whose work Strauss knew to be far superior to his Munich friends', namely that of Gustav Mahler. Before leaving for Munich Strauss had talked Bronsart (who was also President of the Allgemeiner deutscher Musikverein) into scheduling the First Symphony for an 1894 AdMV festival performance in Weimar, and Strauss himself conducted the world premiere of the Second Symphony (without the final movement) as part of a series of guest conducting concerts (1894–95) in Berlin. The fact that Strauss was asked to conduct a series of ten guest concerts (which also included works by Thuille and Schillings) in the German capital only strengthened his position in Munich.

Strauss's major compositional preoccupation during this second Munich period was a return to the tone poem, but these works differed significantly from those before the pivotal *Guntram*. They were significantly longer (*Ein Heldenleben* is nearly three times the length of *Don Juan*), the size of the orchestra increased as well, displaying an increasing pleasure in graphically depicting extra-musical events, and they all address – in one form or another – the relationship between the individual and his outer world, a central theme from *Guntram*. Thus, Till Eulenspiegel confronts the Philistines, the Individual struggles with Nature in *Also sprach Zarathustra*, the tragi-comic Don Quixote battles his way across the Spanish landscape, and the protagonist of *Ein Heldenleben* fights his various adversaries. Yet, this "second cycle" of tone poems begins not unlike the first, in that Strauss returns to a literary theme after the personal, metaphysical *Tod und Verklärung*. Also like the first cycle, the second ends with a non-literary work: *Ein Heldenleben* – the culmination of the nineteenth-century tone poem.

After *Guntram*'s failure, Strauss originally sought to compose another stage work – a light satirical opera to poke fun at provincial narrow-mindedness. The one-act *Till Eulenspiegel bei den Schildbürgern* (1894) never got beyond an incomplete text draft, but in this mythical town of Schilda (a thinly disguised Munich) the hapless, empty-headed townspeople at first sentence Till Eulenspiegel to death, then ultimately make him their mayor. Why Strauss scrapped the opera for a tone poem is not clear, but judging from the composer's own programmatic notes, the symphonic *Till Eulenspiegel* is based on a different scenario: "Once upon a time there was a knavish fool named Till Eulenspiegel. He was a wicked goblin up to new tricks." Then Till rides on horseback through the market, mocks religion (disguised as a cleric), flirts with women, engages in academic double talk with his Philistine audience, and by the end finds himself on a scaffold ready to be hanged. Till Eulenspiegel, unlike the earlier tone poems, lacks the designation Tondichtung in the subtitle; instead, Strauss suggests form rather than genre: "Till Eulenspiegel's Merry Pranks, after the Old Rogue's Tale, set in Rondeau Form for Large Orchestra." One critic suggested that the first prank may well have been the use of the term "rondeau" in the subtitle, for the only real connection with the Old French forme fixe was the composer's choice of spelling. Strauss later described the work as "an expansion of rondo form through poetic content" and looked to the last movement of Beethoven's Eighth Symphony as a model. Given the episodic nature of the work as well as the libertine qualities of its protagonist, Strauss's choice of rondo form is not surprising. But, as in Don Juan, the rondo treatment is hardly conventional, and – also as in Don Juan – seems to be in dialogue with sonata form, which is less unconventional.

Till Eulenspiegel, thus, marks a return to the jocular world of Don Juan, but with a difference, for though the Don was a libertine who had no use for the rules of everyday folk, young Till – with far greater sarcasm – poured scorn on (and even shamed) the narrow-minded world around him. Strauss was so preoccupied with this Eulenspiegel idea that he once again toyed with the idea of a Till opera (this time in five acts), but that impulse would be deferred until the satirical Feuersnot, where the protagonist magician, Kunrad, casts a spell on the provincial citizens of medieval Munich. This growing sense of irony no doubt stemmed from his increasing preoccupation with Nietzsche. Strauss had jettisoned Schopenhauer's pessimism for a Nietzschean optimism dialectically undercut by self-criticism, even by self-doubt. Very much like the young Thomas Mann, Strauss saw in Nietzsche the power of beauty and life, but it is a life constantly thwarted by irony, which though it may woo the intellect, ultimately denies the intellect in favor of life.

The original subtitle of his next tone poem, *Also sprach Zarathustra*, reflects this phenomenon: "Symphonic Optimism in *fin-de-siècle* Form, Dedicated to the 20th Century." "*Fin-de-siècle*," which is intended in a negative or pessimistic sense, thus intentionally thwarts optimism in a vintage Nietzschean manner, where hope and joy are always foiled by disgust and self-doubt. The key to this work may well lie in a throw-away line by Strauss's old Nietzschean friend and *Till Eulenspiegel* dedicatee, Arthur Seidl, who declared – in the first public mentioning of Strauss's new project – that though he was composing a work entitled *Also sprach Zarathustra* the actual subject was taken from Nietzsche's *Human, All Too Human*. This latter work was Nietzsche's first overt rejection of Schopenhauerian metaphysics, especially in its third part, and it may well be that Strauss used the external scaffolding of *Also sprach Zarathustra*, with its colorful, inherently musical aspects (dance and song), informing it with the content of *Human, All Too Human*, which is so laboriously unlyrical and aphoristic.

Strauss later substituted as the subtitle, "Freely after Nietzsche," a description that aptly suggests his liberal treatment of the book's prologue and four sections from which he chose eight of Zarathustra's eighty speeches: "Of Backworldsmen," "Of Great yearning," "Of Joys and Passions," "Funeral Song," "Of Science," "The Convalescent," "The Dance Song," and "The Night Wanderer's Song." Though Zarathustra is a prophet for the *Übermensch*, he well knows that he will never become one; he is a visionary wise enough to realize that he can never purge himself of his metaphysical yearnings. Similar to Amfortas in *Parsifal*, Zarathustra is doomed to eternal convalescence, to self-revulsion and disgust. But Zarathustra, unlike Amfortas, enjoys his convalescence, he revels in eternal recurrence, the inability to transcend. A backward glance at *Tod und Verklärung* shows us just how far from Ritter Strauss had come: in the earlier work the convalescent transcends and is transfigured, symbolized by the movement from C minor to C major. Zarathustra, though he has visions of the next world is always frustrated by self-doubt: C major (which represents Nature) is always just beyond Humanity (represented by B major).

In this way, perhaps, Strauss was truer to Nietzsche than was Mahler, who was likewise preoccupied with the conflict between Humanity and Nature. In the same year as Strauss's tone poem, Mahler set Zarathustra's "Drunken Song of Midnight" in his Third Symphony (and he would revisit this conflict between finite Man and infinite Nature in *Das Lied von der Erde* of 1909). But in contrast to Mahler, Strauss depicts a humanity not in search of eternity, rather one struggling to transcend religious superstition. The beautiful A♭ section ("Of the Backworldsmen") – despite the irresistible beauty of the divided strings, the melodic sweep, the magnificent upward sequential momentum – offers only a parody of religion. Ironic quotations from the Mass ("Credo in unum deum") and later the Magnificat reinforce Strauss's distance from, not identification with his material. Religion is mocked just as sarcastically as when Till Eulenspiegel, dressed as a priest, lampoons religion. Strauss conducted the *Zarathustra* premiere in 1896 with great success. The young Béla Bartók described the work as a "bolt of lightning" that lifted him out of artistic stagnation. The bombastic opening fanfare – trivialized and commodified by popular culture – is Strauss's best-known passage, even if the listener may never have heard of the composer.

Cosima Wagner's reaction to Strauss's new piece was understandably negative, and from 1896 onward an ever-increasing distance grew between the Wagner family and Strauss, who had not been invited back as conductor. Indeed, in early January of that year the composer wrote in his diary that an "unspoken, yet full-fledged split with Wahnfried-Bayreuth" had taken place. The immediate cause was a purported argument between Strauss and Siegfried, but there were a host of other factors ranging from the philosophical (Strauss's separation from the metaphysics of Cosima-style Wagnerism) to the banal (Cosima's disappointment that Strauss had not married her daughter, Eva). Strauss's rising fame and Siegfried's lack of a reputation beyond Bayreuth only made matters worse: Cosima became increasingly defensive about her son, and Strauss saw in Siegfried a modestly talented musician who – because of his name – enjoyed the privilege of conducting in Bayreuth. Still, Cosima was clever enough not to alienate the most successful young composer in Germany, and she even made light of Strauss's modernistic direction in a congratulatory telegram five days after Franz Alexander Strauss's birth on 12 April 1897 (curiously, the first anniversary of Ritter's death): "Hail to the [Strauss] family / please, no Zarathustra as teacher / I offer my own services as governess."[12]

A day before the telegram arrived (16 April 1897), Strauss wrote an entry in his diary: "Symphonic poem *Hero and World* [*Ein Heldenleben*] begins to take shape; as a satyr play to accompany it – *Don Quixote*."[13] Though Nietzsche had attracted Strauss with his affirmative agnosticism and his rejection of Christianity and its "herd morality," the composer was equally compelled by Nietzsche's critical irony, where ideas and concepts quite easily turn on themselves. Thus, it should be no surprise that these next two tone poems, *Don Quixote* and *Ein Heldenleben*, two works that explore the hero and the anti-hero were intended as a pair from the very beginning. The tragicomic *Don Quixote* returns us to the satirical world of *Till Eulenspiegel*, and the subtitle suggests not so much genre (such as *Tondichtung*) as form or procedure: "Fantastic Variations on a Theme of Knightly Character for Large Orchestra."

The question of genre remains elusive, for the work – which features both cello and viola in solo roles – represents a conglomeration of generic and formal paradigms: tone poem, theme and variation, and concerto. Strauss had already written a piece for cello and orchestra (the *Romanza* of 1883), but a more obvious model was Berlioz's *Harold in Italy* (1834). *Don Quixote* features an introduction, ten variations, and a coda that offer, respectively, a portrait of our anti-hero and his faithful Sancho Panza, their ten misadventures, and the death of the Don. Once again Strauss chose selections from a major literary work, and in the tradition of *Don Juan* and *Till Eulenspiegel*, *Don Quixote* unfolds episodically, but these episodes are now more self-contained: as each discrete "chapter" unfolds, so does a new variation. Moreover, this theme-and-variations procedure incorporates nuances of the rondo principle we associate with the two preceding works. Indeed, the themes themselves are rarely varied, rather their musical contexts: a musical analogy of the "hero" and his hapless partner in their different contexts – the adventure with the windmills, the battle with the sheep, the conversation between knight and squire, the adventure with the procession of penitents, the Don's nocturnal vigil over his armor, his meeting with the peasant girl, the "ride" through the air, the journey on the enchanted boat, the battle with the two priests, and Don Quixote's combat with the knight of the shining moon. In the epilogue he returns home where he dies a peaceful death.

The work premiered in March 1898, and the reviews were more mixed than with some of the more recent tone poems. Strauss had now reached a new level in his ability to create concrete sonic images through novel instrumental combinations and juxtapositions: bleating winds and brass to represent sheep, wind machine for the Luftfahrt, snap-pizzicati to evoke the waterlogged adventurers who have just fallen out of their "enchanted boat." Some critics accused Strauss of competing with Cervantes rather than interpreting him; others recognized an increasing aesthetic conflict in his music between technical industry and loftier inspiration, between Strauss the artisan and Strauss the artist. Ernest Newman, who had championed Strauss's earlier work, believed that Strauss had gone too far, reaching the limits of musical onomatopoeia. Rudolf Louis, a Munich music critic and theorist, who had once collaborated with Strauss's old friend Thuille, lamented that the "deictic" Strauss sought to compete with Cervantes himself:

> No musician before now has ever advanced nearly so far in the art of letting the listener see, as it were, with his ears. This is the source of Strauss's unique and personal strength, that he has developed the ideal, elevated gestures of the tonal language of Liszt into a gestural language of great specificity that undertakes quite seriously not only to interpret the events of an external musical plot in tone (by revealing the music that is latent in them) but to draw them until they are recognizable to the inner eye.[14]

Strauss always suggested that Don Quixote and Ein Heldenleben be performed together as a pair, and in fact the earliest musical ideas for Heldenleben emerged while Strauss was working on its predecessor. This early Heldenleben sketch relates to the end of the piece and is labeled "longing for peace after the struggle with the world, refuge in solitude: the Idyll." The parallel with Quixote is obvious, after various struggles the Don – like the Hero – renounces the world and returns home. Cervantes offered Strauss the necessary material with which to explore the anti-hero, but to explore the alternate side Strauss looked to his own life: his love for Pauline, as well as his inner and outer struggles. The six sections of the work – the hero, his adversaries ("internal and external"),[15] his life's companion (Heldensgefährtin), his deeds of war, his works of peace, and his withdrawal from the world – do not go beyond this fundamental idea. Some commentators have seen the work as comprising six continuous sections, but the general contours of sonata form seem more appropriate to Strauss's plan of expository material (hero, adversaries, beloved), developmental space (struggle), and recapitulation (rejecting war, seeking solace in domestic love).

Ein Heldenleben remains Strauss's most controversial work, mainly because its surface elements have been overemphasized. Various critics see the work as a flagrant extension of Strauss's artistic egotism, exemplified by heroic self-portrayal. A deeper look into the meaning of Ein Heldenleben reveals that the issue of autobiography is far more complex than this superficial critique suggests. Ein Heldenleben contains two important themes that show a strong connection to his previous œuvre: first, the Nietzschean struggle between the individual and self-doubt, disgust, resignation and, second, the profundity of domestic love. Essential to this latter preoccupation was his wife Pauline de Ahna. The famous, almost dizzying recollection of themes from previous tone poems, opera, and lieder is based mostly on love themes, related to his "Heldensgefährtin." This culminating effect has a broader context as well, for Ein Heldenleben marks the end of his nineteenth-century tone poems and reflects a composer at the height of his creative powers.

Strauss, who had never been fully at ease with the Munich Opera, received outside offers and solicited some others as well. After 1896, when Levi retired, the triangle of Perfall, Possart, and Strauss grew increasingly tense: the composer had disliked Perfall since his first stint in Munich, and though Strauss maintained friendlier relations with Possart – a popular actor in Munich for whom he had composed the melodrama *Enoch Arden* – he never entirely trusted him as well. And for good reason: both Possart and Perfall continued to hold out hopes that Mottl would come to Munich. It almost looked as if they might get their way in 1897, when Strauss received an offer from Hamburg to replace Mahler, who had left for Vienna. When Hamburg refused to engage Pauline, such a move soon became out of the question; yet another opportunity – a far greater one – emerged within a year when Weingartner stepped down as conductor of the Berlin Court Opera. Strauss, who signed the Berlin contract on 15 April 1898, was offered a handsome salary of 18,000 Marks and a generous pension.

Yet more important than any financial considerations, Strauss knew that his time in Munich had long since run out. Though he appreciated the opportunity of conducting excellent musicians and a fine repertoire, his major focus during these recent years had been composing his tone poems. In short, he had simply outgrown the small circle of friends. Not since Meiningen was Strauss positioned at such a critical moment in his career. Berlin, the busy capital of the young German empire, would offer Strauss a far richer and exciting cultural milieu, where he could explore new artistic directions and meet the important contemporary artists, writers, and intellectuals – personalities that would further stimulate his creativity and career. Most important for Strauss would be an exciting theatrical life unknown in Munich, where he would see the latest plays, some of which had been banned in his *Vaterstadt*, and meet stimulating young directors and playwrights with whom he would ultimately collaborate. Strauss, on the threshold of a new century, would now dedicate his creative life to composing opera, saying farewell to the tone poems of the nineteenth century, to the world of Ritter and the Wagner family, to his family, to the city of his birth that he both hated and loved.

3 The rise of an opera composer

The Berlin that Strauss saw in 1898 was a world-metropolis of nearly 2,000,000 people, the cultural center of modern Germany, and a far cry from the provincial Prussian capital of some 600,000 in 1864, when Strauss was born. This active, burgeoning "Chicago on the Spree" was the ideal antidote to what Strauss perceived as a slow, sleepy, narrow-minded Munich. But as Strauss would soon find out, Berlin was not without its share of philistines, its conservative middle class, especially the reactionary hard line attached to the court of Wilhelm II, who preferred his military marches to concerts and operas. Still, this energetic seat of the young German empire attracted Germany's leading artists and intellectuals, and would stimulate Strauss like no other city, offering the composer a creative environment of unprecedented artistic intensity. The next twenty years – years that brought forth *Salome*, *Elektra*, *Der Rosenkavalier*, *Ariadne auf Naxos*, and *Die Frau ohne Schatten* – would see Strauss reaching the pinnacle of world fame.

Late nineteenth-century Berlin was likened to a giant octopus, sprawling outward into the suburbs, pulling in small neighboring villages with its tentacles. The urban landscape was changing quickly and dramatically. A tram could get from an outlying suburb into the inner city for a concert or play in minutes. Not only had this late industrial age created an affluent business class but, simultaneously, an enormous culture industry with an insatiable appetite for further growth. New philharmonic societies were springing up all over Europe as well as the United States, and subscription concerts were created on an unprecedented scale. Concert and opera guides, designed to make listening easier for a business class with little time to waste, made for great sales at local book shops. For privileged segments of Germany, an overwhelming sense of optimism, even hubris, was in the air. In Berlin this spirit took on a special sense of monumentality, a spirit that flourished not only in urban design, such as the monstrous *Siegesallee*, but in other arts as well, especially music and theater. Between the time of Strauss's birth and his arrival in the German capital the number of theaters tripled, and the number of orchestral ensembles increased significantly as well. Cultural activity was a key indicator of status in the 1890s, something as true in New York, London, or Vienna as it was in Berlin, where this culture-hungry spirit trickled down to a middle class eager to mimic the ways of the rich. No one was more aware of this phenomenon than Richard Strauss, a musician determined to capitalize on this reality.

He presented himself, without apology, as a complete cultural package (the composer who creates, the performer who sells), for there was simply no living musician in the world who could rival the intensity and vitality of his musical activity. Upon arriving in Berlin, Strauss worked with such prodigious energy and in so many different directions that some joked that he must have a secret twin sharing his work. After an inaugural performance of *Tristan* on 5 November 1898, Strauss (who was in the process of scoring *Ein Heldenleben*) went right into action. His diary for the first fortnight went roughly as follows:

Nov. 7   *Heldenleben* two-thirds scored
Nov. 8   *Carmen* (without rehearsal)
Nov. 9   *Hänsel und Gretel* (without rehearsal)
Nov. 12   *Merry Wives of Windsor* (without rehearsal)
Nov. 13   Noontime concert with Halir Quartet, playing Strauss Piano Quartet, Op. 13; evening, Auber's *La Muette de Portici* (with one rehearsal)
Nov. 15   *Fidelio* (without rehearsal)

Nov. 16   *Heldenleben* score eighty pages completed

Nov. 20   *La Muette de Portici*

Nov. 21   Rienzi (without rehearsal)

In the first season alone he conducted twenty-five different operas totaling seventy-one performances, including an ambitious *Ring* cycle in the spring. But this was only part of his career, for during this first year alone he was finishing *Heldenleben*, working on an opera libretto (never to be realized), touring as a guest conductor and lieder accompanist for his wife, while also organizing on behalf of composers' rights.

This ever-active art industry put Strauss in constant demand, and he toured Europe, performing his own works, with unbelievable vigor. Why all this intense self-promotion, especially since Strauss had become an increasingly private man? He wanted, of course, to earn money, but it was money that would assure him – by age fifty – financial independence and, finally, privacy – to be free of any professional responsibilities beyond composing. Time and again he explained his goal to an impatient Pauline, who loathed his hectic touring schedule:

> Money, money, with which I hope soon to come to peace, surrounded by beautiful nature, sunlight, and healthy air, I can peacefully be with you and [Franz] and my little musical notes.[1]

Thus, the fiercely private man forced himself into the role of international, public figure in the ultimate service of seclusion, but it was a seclusion that he never entirely achieved once the two world wars had devastated his earnings. The touring Strauss detested interviews; reporters waiting hours for a meeting with the composer-celebrity would leave disappointed with his one-word or one-line answers. Strauss could be charming and courteous when he had to (when visiting with a head of state or when hosting a party after an opera premiere), but he otherwise preferred the company of his family and a small circle of friends. Strauss's extensive touring, and the attendant health problems, worried his parents, and his father warned that

This senseless behavior will, all too soon, take its revenge on you . . .
You have the opinion that by earning a great fortune now, you can
later live independently only to compose. But do you believe that you
can create anything spiritual with the body of an invalid?[2]

Strauss had stopped heeding his parents long ago, and he kept
pushing onward in various directions. The one direction least related
to music making was his effort on behalf of fellow composers. Upon
his move to Berlin Strauss was searching for a new publisher; his old
publisher and friend, Eugen Spitzweg of Aibl Verlag, could no longer
afford the composer's high fees. Spitzweg had, for example, bought
Aus Italien for 500 Marks, and he had purchased *Don Juan* and *Tod und
Verklärung* for 800 and 1,600 Marks, respectively. Now Strauss hoped
to sell *Heldenleben* for 10,000 Marks, a sum well beyond Spitzweg's
means. It was a time in Germany when musical works were sold for
flat, one-time fees: performing rights, rights to arrangements, and
other uses of a composer's music remained unprotected. With understandable outrage, Strauss recognized an affluent culture industry
where everyone except the composer seemed to be making significant
profits. For that reason he met with the composer Hans Sommer, who
had strong Reichstag connections, and his old schoolmate Friedrich
Rösch, now an attorney, to form a society that would protect the rights
of composers in Germany.[3] Rösch, Sommer, and Strauss spent countless hours writing, organizing, and lobbying for a German copyright
law for music that was finally passed by the Reichstag in 1901, and two
years later the GDT (German Composers' Cooperative) was founded.
It may have been easy for the next generation of German composers to
mock Strauss as "money grubbing," but they were all in his debt for
the royalties they received for their compositions.

For years Strauss had been active in the Allgemeiner deutscher
Musikverein, and in 1901 he was elected its president, the same year
that he took over conducting duties of the Berliner Tonkünstlerverein,
which toured throughout Europe. From 1898 to 1908, as
Hofkapellmeister to the Berlin Opera, Strauss was not allowed to conduct the subscription concerts of the Berlin Philharmonic, led by Felix

Weingartner, although the Tonkünstlerverein position gave Strauss an important venue for conducting orchestral works beyond the consideration of the more conservative Philharmonic. Both appointments of 1901 allowed him to champion music of his contemporaries, including the world premieres of two Mahler symphonies: the Third in 1902 and the Sixth in 1906. Indeed, so much Mahler was performed through the mechanism of the AdMV that it was nicknamed by some in the press as the "Allgemeiner deutscher Mahlerverein."

Once again we face the recurring paradox of *Bürger-vs.-Künstler* in Strauss's personality, for though he enjoyed his comfortable Berlin apartment, and he loyally served his philistine Emperor as court conductor (even dishing up occasional marches to keep him satisfied), his artistic inclinations at the time were at one with the anti-establishment secessionist painters and writers of his day. These were the *fin-de-siècle* modernists who looked to a new art, yet clung to older methods and techniques: Lovis Corinth, Max Liebermann, Slevogt (in the visual arts); Dehmel, Detlev von Liliencron, Frank Wedekind (in literature). Corinth would ultimately design the cover for the score to *Elektra* and Liebermann later created four likenesses of Strauss between 1917–18. Dehmel and Wedekind were particularly interested in having Strauss set their work to music as lieder, ballet, or even opera. Though Strauss set a number of poems by Dehmel and Liliencron, none produced an opera text or ballet scenario that would see fruition.[4]

Strauss ultimately set none of Wedekind's work, but he nonetheless found a kindred spirit in the playwright, with his attacks on repressive Wilhelmine social mores and sexual hypocrisy, and he also strongly sympathized with Wedekind's struggles in Munich to get his works performed. Though banned in Munich, Wedekind's *Erdgeist* premiered in Berlin (1906) with Strauss enthusiastically in attendance. Wedekind earlier had tried to lure Strauss to the musical stage with a racy satirical ballet scenario entitled *Die Flöhe* (The Fleas), where a little insect gets beneath the skirt of a young woman, offering ample opportunity for light-hearted, even slapstick, choreography. The proposed ballet was one of many unrealized projects from the early Berlin period when Strauss was moving away from the role of tone poet, but was not quite sure of his new artistic path. He tried his hand at writing another, less ambitious satirical opera libretto of his own (*Ekke und Schnittlein*), but stopped after two drafts.

Beyond the Wedekind project, Strauss toyed with various other ballet scenarios, among them a proposal by the Austrian poet and playwright Hugo von Hofmannsthal, whom he first met in Berlin in March 1899. Strauss and Hofmannsthal met a second time in Paris a year later, and a fruitful conversation inspired a ballet scenario (*Der Triumph der Zeit*), though Strauss ultimately rejected the plan. He was in the midst of a three-act ballet scenario of his own making (*Kythere*), based on Watteau's *Embarquement pour Cythère* (1719), which he had seen during the 1900 trip to the French capital. It, too, was never realized, though musical sketches were used for various other projects: *Feuersnot*, *Ariadne auf Naxos*, *Bürger als Edelmann*, and *Josephslegende*. Despite his increasing fascination with the stage, Strauss's interest in tone-poem composition was not entirely exhausted: in 1899 he planned a work entitled *Frühling* and in early 1900 he began work on a Nietzschean *Künstlertragödie*, sometimes referred to as "Sunrise" in the diaries, which, though not completed, would find its way into his later *Alpensinfonie*.

During this period Strauss was still smarting from the *Guntram* humiliation in Munich; he wanted his revenge, and it was not until he found something harder-edged, a *Till Eulenspiegel* with a degree of meanness, that he was able to see a major project to the end. He found it in his collaboration with the satirical playwright (and later founder of the Berlin *Überbrettl* cabaret) Ernst von Wolzogen – half-brother of Hans von Wolzogen of the Bayreuth circle. The parallels between Strauss and Wolzogen in 1898 were remarkable: both were brought up in a strict, anti-Wagnerian household, both were agnostic and embraced Nietzsche around the same time, and neither believed in any transcendent redemption through art and the denial of the Schopenhauerian Will. Strauss and Wolzogen were convinced that if there was any possibility of redemption it would not be a denial but an affirmation of the Will: specifically physical sexuality. This conviction, which takes the blatant eroticism of Wagner's *Tristan* as its model, explains a curious 1893 diary entry by Strauss describing the blissful, post-coital expression on a woman's face:

> That smile – I have never seen such [an] expression of the true sensation of happiness! Is not the way to redemption of the Will to be sought here (in the condition of the receiving woman)! . . .
> Affirmation of the will must properly be called affirmation of the body.[5]

Wolzogen and Strauss had both suffered setbacks in Munich, and they were equally eager to get back at the repressed philistines of the Bavarian capital. Strauss, who had already enjoyed fame as a sensualist in the tone poem, now sought to bring sexual material to the stage.

They decided to create a one-act satirical opera, *Feuersnot* (1901), based on the Flemish legend *The Extinguished Fires of Audenaarde*, in which a young man is rejected and humiliated by the woman he tries to woo. He tells his woes to a magician who extinguishes all fire in the town. Only when the (receiving) object of the young man's affection is herself humiliated – a flame magically springs from her backside – can fire be restored. Strauss and Wolzogen moved the setting to Munich, and the magician, not on stage in the operatic version, became a thinly disguised Wagner, the young man, his apprentice, an even more thinly disguised Strauss. "When love is united with the magic of genius," Wolzogen remarked, "even the most annoying Philistine must see the light." Thus, like *Guntram* (but in a different way) *Feuersnot* is unthinkable without Wagner, especially in its numerous tongue-in-cheek quotations, but now Strauss is engaged in the Eulenspiegel-like world of satire as he mocks the citizens of medieval Munich, a setting owing much to *Die Meistersinger von Nürnberg*. But unlike Wagner's *Meistersinger*, redemption comes not through the pure love of a woman, rather from the libidinal flames of physical passion. Given the bizarre sexual content (much of it unstageable),

Feuersnot had trouble with censors from the very beginning, and, given the conservative tastes of the Emperor, a Berlin Court Opera premiere would be out of the question. Ernst von Schuch of the Dresden Staatskapelle agreed to do the job, and the work premiered at the Dresden Royal Opera House on 21 November 1901. Strauss was so pleased with the result that, while he was an active conductor, Schuch would conduct every future Strauss opera premiere.

As disappointed, even angry, as Strauss was that his own Berlin Court Opera would not launch *Feuersnot*, he still enjoyed working and living in Berlin more than any other city. He loved Charlottenburg and the fact that he could be in Grünewald or the theater in a matter of minutes by tram. He delighted in the contrasts between the hectic inner city and the peaceful parks: "Here I can live, cleanly and comfortably. In Munich, on the contrary, one can simply go on existing as a dung beetle if one isn't careful."[6] The fact that his wife did not agree agonized Strauss for years. A proud, patriotic Bavarian general's daughter, Pauline hated everything about Berlin and Prussian life in general; this strong difference of opinion helped cause a major rift in their marriage.

After their vacation at the mountain villa of Pauline's parents in Marquartstein (Bavaria), following Strauss's first Berlin season, Pauline stayed behind with two-year-old Franz, a gesture that deeply hurt Strauss. "End of vacation," he wrote in his engagement calendar (31 August), "return *alone* to Berlin." Ten days later: "The first [wedding] anniversary [spent] *alone*." Though it is not entirely clear how many autumns Richard and Pauline would spend apart, this early Berlin period saw a steadily deteriorating marital relationship. Richard confessed that these "stormy Octobers" were taking their toll on him: "If not much, then at least think a little bit about me, and perhaps ask your heart, for once, and not your thick Bavarian skull (as pretty as it is), then you will receive the right answer."[7] Pauline, whose maternal duties became increasingly demanding, stopped touring with her husband unless she was singing, for the frequent stretches of separation took their toll on her as well. At one point they made preliminary plans for divorce and even drafted a letter (18 October 1901) announcing their separation to Pauline's father, though it was never sent.

This grim context casts curious light on Strauss's cheerful *Symphonia domestica*, conceived in the midst of this marital strife. While vacationing alone in Sandown, Isle of Wight, Strauss sketched out a little scenario for a "Family Scherzo, with Double Fugue, on 3 Themes":

Mein Heim: Ein sinfonisches Selbst- und Familienporträt
[My Home: A Symphonic Self- and Family Portrait]:

Mein Weib, mein Kind, meine Musik
Natur und Sonne, die sind mein Glück.
Ein wenig Gleichmut und viel Humor
Drin thut mir's der Teufel selbst nicht vor!

[My wife, my child, my music
Nature and sun, they are my joy.
A little calm and much humor
There even the devil himself can teach me nothing!]

F major 1st theme: Papa returns from his trip, tired
B major 2nd theme: Mama
D major 3rd theme: Bubi, a mixture, however a greater similarity to
Papa
The three take a walk outdoors. Evening time, cozy family table.
Mama puts Bubi to bed. Papa works. Papa and Mama seul: scène d'amour.
Le Matin: Bubi cries, joyful awakening.
And then a little quarreling and arguing (Mama begins, but Papa ends it),
Reconciliation and cheerful ending.

The very next day Strauss received a bolt from the blue, an angry letter in which Pauline accused him of adultery, demanding an immediate divorce. Pauline, unhappy and jealous when her husband was on tour, routinely opened his mail. One such opened letter, from a Mieze Mücke, read:

8 Strauss and family in Berlin (1904), around the time of *Symphonia domestica*

> Sorry I waited in vain for you yesterday at the Union Bar. Would you
> thus be so friendly and make available a pair of tickets for Monday
> and Wednesday of this week?

Strauss was dumbfounded and entirely innocent, the victim of mistaken identity. But even after he got to the bottom of the mystery – the
letter was intended for the conductor Joseph Stransky (often called
"Straussky" by his friends) – Pauline was not easily assuaged. In a typically Straussian way, the composer would turn this dark, painful
moment in their relationship into material for an autobiographical
comedy years later, his *Intermezzo* of 1923.

After completing *Symphonia domestica*, Strauss sought to distance
himself from its detailed extra-musical ideas, insisting that no program accompany the work at its first performance. In an oft-quoted
(and misused) letter to his friend Romain Rolland, he declared that
"the program is nothing but a pretext for the purely musical expression and development of my emotions, and not a simple musical
description of concrete everyday facts."[8] It is far more likely that
Strauss was placating Rolland, who was bewildered by a banal pro-

gram that he felt diminished an otherwise beautiful work, instead of establishing an artistic manifesto. In different company Strauss boasted that with *Domestica* he had finally reached the point where he was able to differentiate musically between "a knife and a fork." Such a work as *Symphonia domestica*, which is admittedly a purposeful, modern celebration of the everyday, highlights a key artistic preoccupation for Strauss, one that foreshadows many other twentieth-century works to follow, namely the composer's desire to "reveal the profundity inherent in the mundane. . . . in the mundane, ordinary, and intimate there was sufficient ambiguity and poignancy for serious art."[9] It is an anti-metaphysical stance taken to a level that even Nietzsche might not have recognized. When asked to justify this glorification of the banal, the everyday, Strauss responded: "What could be more serious than married life? Marriage is the most profound event in life and the spiritual joy of such a union is heightened by the arrival of a child. [Married] life naturally has its humor, which I also injected into this work in order to enliven it."[10] His preoccupation with marital relationships, especially the issue of fidelity, would form a vital bond between Strauss and his future librettist, Hugo von Hofmannsthal.

Symphonia domestica premiered, not in Germany or even Europe for that matter, but rather at Carnegie Hall in New York City, the centerpiece of his first North American concert tour in 1904. Though Strauss well realized that he was likely the most famous living composer, he seemed genuinely surprised at the enthusiastic welcome that he received in the New World. In two months he and his wife gave concerts and recitals in New York, Pittsburgh, Milwaukee, Detroit, Cincinnati, Buffalo, and Chicago. In Chicago Strauss was able to repay the debt he owed Theodore Thomas, who had premiered his Second Symphony in New York in 1884. The greatest scandal of the trip were two concerts that Strauss conducted in a makeshift auditorium of Wanamaker's department store. Such concerts were not unusual in large American department stores at the time, but the German press was indignant, and a host of angry columns appeared all over Germany. Rumors that Strauss had sold out to crass American business interests soon got out of hand: one article even declared that Wanamaker's – not Carnegie Hall – had been the site for *Symphonia domestica*'s premiere. Sell-out or not, Strauss was treated like a visiting head of state all over the United States; shortly before the composer returned to Europe, Theodore Roosevelt invited him to the White House.

Even before completing *Domestica*, with its harmless depiction of bourgeois family life, the protean Strauss was already sketching an entirely different project, an opera that would combine oriental exoticism and sexual depravity: *Salome* (1905). Scandal and censorship were the norm in the world of modern art in the early twentieth century, and *Salome* was no exception. *Feuersnot*, though favorably received, failed to catch on beyond Germany, given its strong local color and often impenetrable Bavarian dialect. Strauss was a composer of international stature only in the realm of lieder and orchestral music, but all this changed after *Salome* premiered in Dresden on 9 December 1905. Lust, incest, decapitation, and necrophelia joined forces with sinuous chromaticism and dazzling orchestration to create a work that provoked as much fascination as revulsion. *Salome* was, in short, an overnight international opera sensation that within its first two years was performed all over Germany as well as in Austria, Czechoslovakia, Italy, Belgium, Switzerland, France, Holland, Poland, and the United States.

That Strauss was on his way to becoming the world's leading opera composer surprised no one who knew him. He had quickly immersed himself in Berlin's active theatrical world. Word had got round that Strauss was looking for a one-act companion work for *Feuersnot*, and proposals poured in from playwrights eager for quick international recognition. Strauss himself was in no hurry; he was finishing the score to *Domestica* and in the midst of composing his gigantic, and rarely performed, *Taillefer* (1903) for orchestra, chorus, and soloists. In January 1902, Anton Lindner (editor of the *Wiener Rundschau* and author of the poem "Hochzeitlich Lied," set by Strauss in 1898) sent the composer a copy of Oscar Wilde's *Salome*, a first edition translated by Hedwig Lachmann containing ten striking illustrations by Marcus Boehmer.

Lindner, hoping for another collaboration with Strauss, promised that a libretto version would soon follow. Two months later all Strauss got was an apology from Lindner who decided that the whole thing would have to be redone from top to bottom, and he sent a sample of some verse treatments of the play, which failed to impress the composer. Everything changed after the Berlin premiere of Wilde's *Salome* in November 1902. Directed by the young, innovative Max Reinhardt with the stunning Gertrude Eysoldt in the title role, *Salome* mesmerized Strauss, who returned to see it again two months later. By then he had resolved to forget about Linder's awkward verse and set the play itself to music. A look at Strauss's cuts and annotations in his copy of the play shows a composer who knew precisely what he wanted.

Strauss worked quickly, eliminating some forty percent of the dialogue, accentuating the text's contrasting images as well as its symmetry: Herod, Jochanaan, the Jews; Salome's three seduction songs with Herod's three persuasive speeches; Salome's ostinato "Ich will den Kopf des Jochanaan!"; and of course her erotic dance of the seven veils. Strauss, with his tremendous instincts for the musical stage, successfully streamlined the text to create an effective sense of escalation culminating in Salome's disturbing final monologue, where she becomes increasingly detached from the outer world. With tongue in cheek, Strauss remarked that after the fact it was easy to say that Wilde's play was "crying out for music." Still, he wryly added, "that [music] had to be discovered." The unprecedented speed at which it was composed (first sketches in July 1903, final sketches September 1904) suggests that whatever ideas he was digging for were already close to the surface.

Had Strauss become famous or infamous as an opera composer of international note? *Salome* – Strauss's first *Literaturoper* – would inevitably be drawn into a more general discussion of the composer's literary tastes. Even some of his most loyal supporters (Romain Rolland,

Ernest Newman, Oscar Bie) believed Strauss had gravely erred in his choice of textual subject. Rolland, who likewise found Domestica to be inappropriate (but for reasons of triviality) feared that Strauss had been drawn into the solipsistic thrall of a brilliant but unhealthy "decadent literature":

> [Salome] is a meteor, the power and brilliancy of which commands the attention of everyone, even those who don't like it . . . I saw a well-known French musician, who hated it, but who had just heard it for the third or fourth time . . . I don't think that one could find a more manifest proof of your power . . . the greatest in Europe today.[11]

We do not know whether or not Strauss replied to Rolland, but far from being ashamed by what he had done, he clearly delighted in the scandal. The anti-bourgeois fire in his bourgeois soul was still burning, and he should hardly have been surprised that the Metropolitan Opera canceled performances or that Mahler failed to get it past the Viennese censors. A new military march and a special performance of Kaiser Wilhelm's beloved Der Freischütz under Strauss helped clear the way for the Berlin premiere, where a glimmering Star of Bethlehem in the distance was a required part of the staging just before the fall of the curtain. It was admittedly a gratuitous gesture, for the "dangerous" fin-de-siècle femme fatale has already been safely eliminated under the shields of Herod's guards. The audience could then go home assured that society's values, hypocritical as they may have been, would ultimately prevail. Thus, with great skill, Strauss the bourgeois revolutionary could titillate, even offend the middle class without alienating it. What Theodor Adorno criticized in Wagner seems applicable here as well, namely that "[Strauss] violates the taboos of the bourgeois work-ethic, but his blessing redounds to the glory of his benefactors."[12]

Salome's success gave Strauss great confidence as a composer for the theater, and in addition enough capital (Fürstner paid 60,000 Marks to publish the score) to build a Bavarian villa of his own. Given Strauss's hectic schedule, summer offered him the only time for seri-

ous, sustained creative work (fall and winter were mostly for orchestrating), and he regularly spent his summers between 1890 and 1908
composing. Young Franz was nine years old, and his parents sought
the privacy of their own summer home. The land, in Garmisch, was
purchased in June 1906 and extensive negotiations were made with
the famed Munich architect Emmanuel Seidl. By the next summer
construction had begun, and all was completed by June 1908.

After *Salome*, it had become fairly clear that Strauss preferred composing adjacent operas of powerful contrasts: the ponderous *Guntram*
was followed by the farcical *Feuersnot*, in turn followed by the serious,
yet bizarre *Salome*, which, according to Strauss had exhausted his
"tragic vein." But in autumn 1905, after seeing Hofmannsthal's *Elektra*
(again, directed by Reinhardt and also featuring Eysoldt in the title
role), Strauss dropped his initial plans for a comedy. Where Strauss
was immediately struck by the textual imagery in Wilde's play, *Elektra*
appealed to him on a far more physical, gestural level. Wilde, the *fin-
de-siècle* modernist, had used an old language to express new ideas,
while Hofmannsthal increasingly found that very language to be
increasingly inadequate to express the ideas of a new century. He
rejected the solipsistic poetry of his youth and discovered that modern
language in theater, *Elektra* being his first significant venture in this
new genre.

The solution, thus, would be found in gesture, and in *Elektra*, a
Freudian interpretation of Sophocles' tragedy, Strauss was riveted by
the use of body motion (so effectively directed by Reinhardt), the con-
centration of plot action, and the steadily-rising tension culminating
in Elektra's dance after her father's (Agamemnon's) murder has been
avenged. This opera was unprecedented in its elemental emotional
power – no contemporary work had probed such psychological
depths, created such awesome climaxes, or exploited such a vast
orchestral ensemble. If the audience was scandalized after *Salome* it
was utterly shocked by *Elektra*, which, however, failed to outshine her
flashier sister opera. Yet, very much like her predecessor, *Elektra* –
despite the visual and aural violence – ultimately affirms society's

9 The Strausses' 1908 villa in Garmisch, as it appears today

values. Elektra, too, must die for the good of her community, or, in the simplest terms, for the good of the audience. During her wild, solo, maenadic dance (hearing a music that no one else hears), she calls for others to join, but they stand aside, horrified by what they see.

Composer and playwright met on 22 February 1906 in Berlin, and Strauss received permission from a delighted Hofmannsthal to use his text as he saw fit. Though the two had briefly met twice before, this Berlin meeting was the first one of significance, and Hofmannsthal would become the most important figure in Strauss's life since Alexander Ritter; their artistic collaboration was to span more than two decades. But not long after this meeting, Strauss hesitated, seeing too many parallels between the two tragic plays: both works feature a strong female protagonist consumed by an *idée fixe*; both culminate in dance; and both heroines are finally undone by their own neurotic fixations. A comedy was needed before he could confront the Elektra material. But, after much persuasion, Hofmannsthal kept him on course, and by June he was composing.

Strauss's experience in cutting and shaping the Wilde play served him well with Hofmannsthal's text, and, with great speed, he created a remarkable libretto that focused almost entirely on Elektra, her mother (Klytämnestra), and sister (Chrysothemis). The composer further enhanced the arch-like shape of the play, the keystone being the central confrontation between Elektra and Klytämnestra. It is the tensest scene that Strauss ever composed and certainly the most daring in its hyper-chromatic language that often borders on atonality. If *Elektra* is performed less often than *Salome*, it is because it is Strauss's most difficult soprano role. The title soprano is on stage for every scene save one, and she must do constant battle with a tumultuous orchestra, which proudly displays an ardent, young composer's contrapuntal, leitmotivic skill. Years later Strauss was embarrassed that much of the singing was, as he put it, "handicapped by instrumental polyphony," and he later suggested, lightheartedly, that it should be conducted in the manner of Mendelssohn: "fairy music."

While orchestrating *Elektra*, Strauss had gained enough prestige in Berlin to be appointed *Generalmusikdirektor* in April 1908, and more important he was granted a year's leave (without salary) for the next season, during which time he succeeded Weingartner as director of the prestigious Berlin Philharmonic subscription concerts. Strauss completed the score a couple of weeks before his leave from the Berlin Opera began, a time that marked a vital period of relative repose, allowing the composer to ponder in what form and in what direction his creative energies should go. Worn out by the strident twin tragedies, Strauss was ultimately determined to compose a full-fledged comedy, and he believed that Hofmannsthal would have a Casanova-based comedy (*Christinas Heimreise*) ready for him sometime that autumn.

The vicissitudes of the Casanova project taught Strauss much about working with a writer of such high literary stature and independence of mind. This was their first collaborative effort, and Hofmannsthal especially had trouble thinking of his three-act comedy purely as material destined for music. He decided that it would first have to be written as a spoken play then be fashioned as a libretto, and much to Strauss's disappointment, a libretto never emerged. The industrious composer saw his sabbatical slipping away without a major project in the pipeline. Remarkably, however, all that changed in a few months, for on 11 February 1909 Hofmannsthal was in Weimar with his friend Harry Graf Kessler:

> I have spent three quiet afternoons here drafting the full and entirely original scenario for an opera, full of burlesque situations and characters, with lively action, pellucid almost like a pantomime. There are opportunities in it for lyrical passages, for fun and humor, even for a small ballet . . . It contains two big parts, one for a baritone and another for a graceful girl dressed up as a man, à la Farrar or Mary Garden. Period: the old Vienna under the Empress Maria Theresa.[13]

Who would have thought from this little aside in a letter concerning the Casanova comedy that Strauss was about to compose his most famous opera? Three days later Strauss and Hofmannsthal met in Berlin to discuss the new scenario, and a follow-up discussion took place in Vienna a month later, when Strauss was in town for the Vienna premiere of *Elektra*. At last he had found his librettist, his "da Ponte and Scribe rolled into one," and he had a text that seemed to "set itself to music like oil and melted butter."[14] By May an ecstatic Strauss was already composing, and told Hofmannsthal that his work was flowing "like the Loisach," a Bavarian alpine river.

This time it was neither Mendelssohn's "fairy music," nor the crashing dissonance of *Elektra* that would permeate his new opera, but rather the world of Mozart. Though the libretto bears an intentional resemblance to da Ponte's *Marriage of Figaro*, it conflates a far wider range of sources, including Beaumarchais, Molière, Hogarth, and even parts of Wagner's *Meistersinger*. What had inspired Strauss, the lover of contrasts and juxtapositions, were the conflations of comic elements with those of significant profundity. In order to realize such a wide range of emotions Strauss developed a musical language more complex and challenging than *Salome*'s chromaticism

10 Cartoon lampooning Strauss's fourth opera, *Elektra* (1909)

and *Elektra*'s dissonance, for what Strauss sought in *Der Rosenkavalier* was a critical layering of musical styles (Mozart, Johann Strauss, Verdi, and others). Taking a step well beyond the old-fashioned, decadent, *fin-de-siècle Salome*, Strauss realized that the musical language for the new century should be one that intentionally lacks stylistic uniformity, a language that reflects a modernist preoccupation with the dilemma of history, one that arguably foreshadows the dissolution of the ideology of style in the late twentieth century. Through the lens of *Rosenkavalier*, with its ahistorical anachronisms, we may see a composer who keenly recognized the disunities of modern life and believed that such incongruities should not be masked by a unified musical style.

Der *Rosenkavalier* is a work about time and transformation on multiple levels, and this transformative theme was an element close to Strauss as early as *Death and Transfiguration* and as late as his final instrumental work, the *Metamorphosen*. The first transformation in *Der Rosenkavalier* begins with the very opening lines, "What you were, what you are – that nobody knows, that no one can explain," when Octavian changes the verb "to be" from the past to the present tense. Later in the act Baron Ochs boasts that he is "Jupiter blessed with a thousand forms," but Octavian himself is the one who takes on various transformations throughout the opera: as the Marschallin's adolescent lover, as her chambermaid, as a rose cavalier, and – by the end – as a wiser young man.

To Hofmannsthal the miracle of life is that an old love can die, while a new one can arise from its ashes. Yet in this transformation, which requires us to forget, we still preserve our essence. How is it that – in the same body – we are what we once were, now are, and will become? This great mystery of life is, in one way or another, a theme that permeates most of Hofmannsthal's work. The Marschallin ponders this enigma in her poignant monologue ending Act I, one of the opera's great moments in both score and libretto. Beyond the monologue, Rosenkavalier's delightfully anachronistic nineteenth-century waltzes, the magical presentation of the rose in Act II, and the sublime final trio of Act III remain some of Strauss's best loved music. Yet their popularity, independent of the operatic whole (in the form of recorded excerpts or concert performances), has also overshadowed the theatrical brilliance of this modern stage work by Strauss.

There is yet another element that sets Der Rosenkavalier apart from all previous operas by Strauss. For the first time, even since the days of the tone poems, we have a work that is not preoccupied with the post-Nietzschean notion of an individual in struggle with his or her outer world. This subject-object duality is to be found in all of the nineteenth-century tone poems and, significantly, in the first four operas as well: Guntram struggles with his fraternal order and ultimately abandons it; in Feuersnot the visionary outsider, Kunrad, punishes the narrow-minded citizens of medieval Munich; Salome loathes Herod and his court, withdrawing into her own delusional reality; and Elektra (who, likewise, hates her stepfather) lives in her solitary world of revenge, ostracized by her community. Indeed, so complex is the libretto to Der Rosenkavalier that it is difficult to say who the lead character actually is. Until three months before the premiere the title was

Ochs von Lerchenau, thought by both collaborators to be the main character, and though Octavian is technically the title role, his guise – not
his actual name – is given as the title. And, of course, many have
argued that although she does not appear in the second act and only
towards the end of the third, the Marschallin's spirit threads its way
throughout the entire work.

Strauss and Hofmannsthal knew they had created a different type
of work for the stage, one that would require singers with unique
acting abilities, and they realized in advance how difficult rehearsals
would be in Dresden. In the first place, they failed to get their Ochs of
choice, Friedrich Mayr, and had to settle for the stiff, leaden Carl
Perron. Worse yet was the Dresden Opera producer, Georg Toller,
who had shown such modest production insights in the Elektra premiere. But Hofmannsthal devised ways of getting around the problem. He made sure that the stage design would be carried out by Alfred
Roller, the famed designer from Vienna who had worked so successfully with Mahler. Roller had written out a highly detailed production
book, in close consultation with Hofmannsthal, that was unprecedented by operatic standards. Moreover, Hofmannsthal made sure
that his friend from Berlin, Max Reinhardt, would be on hand to offer
advice, even if it meant that, at first, he was not permitted to stand on
the stage where Toller served as the official producer. In those vexing
early rehearsals Reinhardt had to offer advice from the wings or in a
huddled corner, and his name did not appear on the program.

"It is horrible" was the terse description in Strauss's calendar on
the day of the first rehearsal. Hofmannsthal described that grim day in
far greater detail: "How sad we were after the first lamentable rehearsals, how helpless and sad. I feel so sorry for Strauss, the great strong,
part coarse, part over-refined man who was so near tears. Without
Max Reinhardt we would have been driven to despair." A week of tire-
less work by Reinhardt and Roller put Hofmannsthal in a far brighter
frame of mind, one that enjoyed "those beautiful, long morning
orchestral rehearsals where we stood above watching the colorful
stage design . . . It is remarkable how seldom one is brought to tears by

11 Strauss (right) with Hugo von Hofmannsthal, Austrian poet, playwright, and
Strauss's finest long-standing librettist. Garmisch 1911

whole beauty, by a complete unity, by absolute harmony. I remember
such an experience the first time I saw the Elgin Marbles and one time
when I stood before a landscape, before the Gulf of Ithea."[15] This was
the first and last time that Hofmannsthal believed a complete synthesis of poetry, music, and acting had been achieved.

Events surrounding the Dresden premiere followed a pattern set by
Elektra two years earlier, namely the creation of a massive publicity
campaign, but one that kept the press at a distance: they were allowed
neither to attend rehearsals nor to have piano-vocal scores at their dis-
posal. No one knew the complexities of the culture industry better
than Strauss, who – though he disliked the press – knew how to
exploit it; even months before the premiere newspaper "rumor"
bulletins concerning *Rosenkavalier* appeared with remarkable regular-
ity. By now Dresden had been dubbed Strauss's Bayreuth, and the
shops that had sold *Elektra* boots, spoons, and beer mugs just two
years earlier were now stocked with various *Rosenkavalier* memora-
bilia. The premiere was, in short, an international sensation, but one
where the audience first seemed to be more enthusiastic about the
work than the critics, who were mostly baffled by the stylistic contrasts, especially the anachronistic use of waltzes. After the premiere,
Strauss and Hofmannsthal were regaled at a gala dinner for more than
400 guests at the Hotel Bellevue. The next evening saw a premiere in
Nuremberg and in a little over three weeks performances took place in
Munich, Mainz, Zurich, and Hamburg. The greatly anticipated
Vienna premiere, featuring the Ochs of choice, Friedrich Mayr, took
place on 8 April 1911, and the banquet that followed included nearly all
the leading figures of Viennese musical and literary life.

Sadly that list did not include Gustav Mahler, who was in a Paris
clinic suffering from a terminal bacterial infection. Within a month,
indeed just six days after his return to Vienna, he would be dead.
Strauss was at home in Garmisch and wrote in his calendar:

> Gustav Mahler passed away following a grave illness. The death of
> this aspiring, idealistic, energetic artist [is] a heavy loss . . . Mahler,
> the Jew, could achieve elevation in Christianity. As an old man the
> hero Wagner returned to it under the influence of Schopenhauer. It is
> clear to me that the German nation will achieve new energy only by
> liberating itself from Christianity . . . I shall call my alpine symphony:
> *Der Antichrist*, since it represents: moral purification through one's
> own strength, liberation through work, worship of eternal,
> magnificent nature.[16]

The death of Mahler had reawakened a Nietzschean spirit in Strauss that had lain dormant for over a decade. Though Strauss admired Mahler and Wagner, he nonetheless lamented their unshakable allegiance to Schopenhauer, whose philosophy – at least to Strauss's thinking – saw the transcendent space of spirituality as the ultimate refuge, as the final resistance to the primal forces of the Will. Strauss's early choice of title was no doubt inspired by Nietzsche's 1888 essay *Der Antichrist*, which was published in 1895, a year before Strauss's *Also sprach Zarathustra*. The *Alpensinfonie*, Strauss's final symphonic poem, went through the longest gestation period of any of his symphonic works, dating back to 28 January 1900, when he planned to compose a tone poem called *Der Sonnenaufgang* (Sunrise). On 11 July, when he began sketching, he called the work *Eine Künstlertragödie (Der Sonnenaufgang)*, and the original scenario consisted of two parts:

1. An artist who, despite his joy in creation, suffers from doubt (as did Zarathustra and the Hero of *Heldenleben*) and is comforted by his lover, who spurs him on to new creative work.
2. The catastrophe, where their "love-madness" ultimately leads to ruin and death.

The setting for this work is the Alps, and the struggle between the artist and his natural surroundings plays a fundamental role in the shaping of this work. The parallels between the *Artist's Tragedy*, *Also sprach Zarathustra*, and *Ein Heldenleben* are obvious (struggles with nature, doubt, and the artist's/hero's companion), but less obvious and equally compelling is the connection with Strauss's earlier *Wandrers Sturmlied* (Goethe), where in a raging storm the poet wanders, thinking of his former love, asking not God but Genius to protect him from the forces of nature.

After Mahler's death Strauss worked more extensively on his *Antichrist* symphony (soon to become *Eine Alpensinfonie*), incorporating important elements of the *Künstlertragödie*, especially the opening at sunrise. The work was completed in short score by 1913 and in full score by 1915, and, as in *Zarathustra*, Strauss does not portray the finite Individual jealous of eternal Nature but rather one who celebrates –

12   The Dresden Opera, where nine of Strauss's fifteen operas were premiered

who is inspired to do great deeds by his natural environment. In an unpublished diary entry on the *Alpensinfonie*, shortly after its premiere, Strauss stresses that both Judaism and Christianity – in short, metaphysics – are unhealthy and unproductive; they are incapable of embracing Nature as a primary, life-affirming source.

As Nietzschean as all this sounds, Strauss ultimately did not choose the philosopher's *Antichrist* essay as his paratextual model; instead he turned to the very alpine landscape that surrounded his home in Garmisch. The ascent and descent from an alpine mountain serve as a metaphor for this exaltation of nature. Strauss's *Zarathustra* and the *Alpensinfonie* both begin at sunrise, and in the latter work the composer specified twenty-three tableaux along this twenty-four-hour journey:

Night, Sunrise, Ascent, Entry into the Forest, Wandering by the Brook, By the Waterfall, Apparition, On the Flowering Meadows, On the Pastures, Through the Thicket and Briar, On the Glacier, Dangerous Moment, On the Summit, Vision, Mists Arrive, The Sun Gradually Darkens, Elegy, Calm before the Storm, Tempest and Storm, Descent, Sunset, Echo, and Night.

Despite its philosophical roots, *Eine Alpensinfonie* strikes one as out-wardly unphilosophical, proclaiming with startling beauty the glories of the natural world. *Eine Alpensinfonie* is unprecedented in Strauss's output both in terms of duration (fifty minutes) and size (requiring over 140 players if one includes offstage horns, trumpets, and trom-bones). Critical reaction after the October 1915 premiere was mixed; some went as far as to describe it negatively as "cinema music," a pre-scient claim, given that Germany was on the verge of a cinematic revo-lution that would commence shortly after the First World War.

A major reason for the lengthy gestation period of the *Alpensinfonie* was Strauss's preoccupation with projects he considered more important or more pressing. Indeed, months before Mahler's death he considered the direction his next operatic collaboration with Hofmannsthal should take, convinced that it should be a return to tragedy. Hofmannsthal faithfully supplied him with the scenario for *Das steinerne Herz* (The Stone Heart), an opera to be based on the theme of a "heart that beats and a heart that is frozen," where a poor man of the woods exchanges his heart for one made of stone in order to acquire wealth and power, and by the end he begs that his heart – his humanity – be returned. These folk-tale themes of acquiring and losing one's humanity ultimately would find their way into *Die Frau ohne Schatten* (1918). But the poet found it difficult to immerse himself in that world; he remained preoccupied with the stylized aura of the eighteenth century, especially the work of Molière, which had partly inspired the *Rosenkavalier* libretto. The immediate result was *Ariadne auf Naxos* (1912), a theatrical hybrid combining spoken theater (an arrangement of the Molière-inspired *Le bourgeois gentilhomme* with incidental music) and opera.

Neither Strauss nor Hofmannsthal had any idea that *Ariadne* – orig-inally planned as a short, interim work – would become such a com-plex and time-consuming collaboration. This was the first real test of their relationship and a source of friction from its earliest stages in January 1911 to the premiere in October 1912, the revision of *Ariadne* in 1916, and the revised *Bürger als Edelmann* a year later. Strauss was an assiduous composer, and he worked methodically, preferring to have his summer's compositional project settled by early spring. Without his tragic libretto in hand, Strauss wrote Hofmannsthal on 17 March: "Don't forget, I've still got no work for the summer. Writing symphonies doesn't amuse me any longer. I hope you're working vigorously!" But just as with *Christinas Heimreise*, Hofmannsthal was having trouble seeing his *Steinernes Herz* as a viable libretto; the more he thought about it, the more complex the work became, and he resolved not to begin writing the libretto until everything had ripened fully in his mind.

In the meantime he was thinking more about Molière and the possibility of a hybrid work that would combine theater, dance, singing, and mime. Despite his pleasure with *Rosenkavalier*, Hofmannsthal felt that his libretto had been swamped by music at critical moments, and he wanted to ensure the integrity of those separate elements in *Ariadne* from the outset by making them a critical part of the libretto. His initial idea was a two-act arrangement of Molière's five-act *Bourgeois gentilhomme*, a play that would include the opera *Ariadne auf Naxos* as a *divertissement* at the end (the work ended up being the Molière, with incidental music, followed by the opera after an intermission). Strauss was hesitant at first, failing to understand how central this project was to Hofmannsthal's artistic development.

Hofmannsthal designed *Ariadne* specifically for Max Reinhardt and his Deutsches Theater in Berlin, a project that was an extension of ideas that had originated around the turn of the century. This was that critical period of artistic pessimism in Hofmannsthal's life, when he turned his back on the very genre (lyric poetry) that had brought him such early celebrity. It was a time of both inner reflection and exploration, a search for a mode of expression beyond mere words, which he began to distrust as the sole bearer of expressive or emotional content. Instead, he sought a language more immediate than what is spoken or written: "neither Latin nor English, neither Italian nor Spanish, but a language none of whose words is known to me."[17] It could never be found in poetry, but rather in the discourse of theater, in a fusion (but not a synthesis) of the arts: acting, gesture, ritual,

myth, scene design, and ultimately music. The significance of
Reinhardt's guidance during this critical stage in Hofmannsthal's
career around 1903 cannot be overstated, and as we know from
Rosenkavalier he remained an important influence. Indeed, while
working on *Ariadne*, which was dedicated to Reinhardt,
Hofmannsthal insisted that "wild horses will not get me to carry out
[*Ariadne*] . . . unless Reinhardt is to produce it; I say this not for senti-
mental reasons, but because the whole bizarre piece of work can only
exist in the special atmosphere of Reinhardt's theater for which it is
designed."[18]

That Strauss failed to understand this "bizarre piece of work" is
clear from letters early on in the collaboration, and the composer's
lack of comprehension increasingly annoyed Hofmannsthal. For the
first time, these opposing personalities – the sensible Bavarian, the
sensitive Viennese – clashed. The composer required a concrete
notion of what musical moments lay in the libretto, and he outlined
them for Hofmannsthal as best he could:

1. Recitative and aria for Ariadne
2. Harlekin's song
3. Zerbinetta's coloratura aria
4. Male quartet for Harlekin and company, becoming a quintet with
   Zerbinetta
5. Buffo male trio
6. Finale: Naiad's warning, duet of Zerbinetta and Ariadne
   (concluding with Bacchus' entry), love duet (Ariadne and Bacchus),
   final ensemble

But Strauss still needed to understand this work; he found it difficult
to compose for abstractions, for stylized figures, and Hofmannsthal
fulfilled the composer's wishes in a remarkable letter of mid-July 1911,
which – following Strauss's suggestion – was published shortly
before the premiere. He wrote:

> What [*Ariadne*] is all about is one of the straightforward and
> stupendous problems of life: fidelity; whether to hold fast to that

which is lost, to cling to it even in death – or to live, to live on, to get over it, to transform oneself, to sacrifice the integrity of the soul and yet in this transmutation to preserve one's essence, to remain a human being and not to sink to the level of beast, which is without recollection.[19]

Some lines from the opera, sung by the Composer to Zerbinetta, reflect this theme so central to Hofmannsthal:

> [Ariadne] is the woman who does not forget. She gives herself to Death – is no longer there – disappears – throws herself into the mystery of transformation – is born anew – born again in [Bacchus'] arms. Then he becomes a god! How else in the world could one become a god except through this experience?

Hofmannsthal finally articulated a topic that resonated with the composer, emphasizing the theme central to the previous opera: that of transformation on its various levels. Through Ariadne's love, Bacchus is transfigured, and Ariadne who longs for death as she awaits the unfaithful Theseus, is herself transformed by embracing Bacchus and accepting life. And, of course, Strauss savored the juxtapositions, the intersections of *opera seria* with those of *commedia dell'arte*, where moments of grandeur are undercut by the coquettish Zerbinetta, the composer's favorite character.

Ariadne auf Naxos is another opera in Strauss's new modern vein, yet its critical stylistic multilayerings and its sense of parody are even more sharply delineated than its predecessor. The opera forges a new relationship between composer, performer, and audience, for without the audience's knowledge of tradition, parody cannot function. If in *Rosenkavalier* Strauss alludes to the style of other composers, *Ariadne* quotes specific musical works: Harlekin's song ("Lieben, Hassen, Hoffen, Zagen") is based on the opening theme of Mozart's A major piano sonata K. 331, and the melody of the Nymphs' trio ("Töne, töne, süsse Stimme") comes from Schubert's *Wiegenlied* ("Schlafe, schlafe, holder, süsser Knabe"). Although Zerbinetta's famous coloratura aria makes no direct quotations, Strauss's letters to

13 Max Reinhardt: one of the great theater directors of the early twentieth century
and a central figure in the Strauss–Hofmannsthal collaboration

Hofmannsthal make it clear from the outset that he looked to Bellini,
Donizetti, and others as stylistic models.

The original conception that featured *Le bourgeois gentilhomme* as
play followed by the opera *Ariadne auf Naxos* (which itself juxtaposed
the worlds of *opera seria* and *commedia dell'arte*) did not succeed. After

the Stuttgart premiere of 1912, the entire work was revised. By 1916, composer and librettist had replaced the play with a lively operatic prologue, presenting a behind-the-scenes view of the operatic stage, followed by the opera itself. The work's juxtaposition and fragmentation of elements (e.g. the everyday world of the Prologue vs. the loftier Opera) present a complex amalgam of contrasting literary and musical styles that, at face value, appear to undermine the overall coherence of the work. In the hands of lesser artists, uniting these jarring contrasts could have proved an impossible task. But Strauss's penchant for juxtaposing the trivial and the exalted made him the ideal match for Hofmannsthal's chief aim in *Ariadne*, namely to "build on contrasts, to discover, above these contrasts, the harmony of the whole." The opera would be the first of many twentieth-century operas (such as those by Busoni, Weill, and others) to be based on *commedia dell'arte* over the next couple of decades.

Strauss's incidental music for the Molière play was not wasted; rather it was used in a revised version of the play that included pantomime and dance. *Der Bürger als Edelmann* premiered in Berlin in 1918, although the incidental music is heard most often as part of an orchestral suite, which was first performed two years later. Gesture and dance were two modes of artistic expression central to both Strauss and his collaborator. Indeed, Hofmannsthal's very first letter to the composer (11 November 1900) proposed the ballet scenario *Der Triumph der Zeit*, but Strauss was already at work on his own ballet, *Kythere*, which was never finished. Thus it was probably inevitable that Hofmannsthal, who viewed gesture as the purest form of communication, would ultimately approach Strauss with another ballet proposal, first *Orest und die Furien*, which Strauss rejected in 1912 and then *Josephslegende*, which was proposed the same year.

The Joseph project, which included the significant collaboration of Hofmannsthal's friend Harry Graf Kessler, was to be realized by Diaghilev's *Ballets russes*, with Vaslav Nijinsky in the title role and choreography by Mikhail Fokine. Strauss had enjoyed seeing the *Ballets russes* in Berlin and, of course, had been searching for a proper ballet scenario since his first year in the German capital. The composer was excited by the prospect of writing ballet music to be realized by the great Nijinsky, but by the time of the premiere Nijinsky had fallen out with the company, and the Paris premiere of 1914 featured the lesser Leonid Massine in the role of Joseph. The exotic, oriental extravagance of *Josephslegende* recalls *Salome*, as does the erotic conflict between the chaste Joseph and the sensual *femme-fatale* Potiphar's Wife. The score, which incorporates material from Strauss's unfinished *Kythere*, foreshadows some of the more exotic moments in *Die Frau ohne Schatten*, especially in its timbral qualities, with the use of harp, celeste, and triple-divided first violins. Strauss, now age fifty, conducted the premiere in Paris on 14 May 1914, having just been awarded officer rank in the French Legion of Honor. That night Strauss's beloved conductor Ernst von Schuch – who premiered four of Strauss's operas (*Feuersnot* through *Der Rosenkavalier*) – died in Dresden.

Other honors poured in that summer for the fifty-year-old Strauss, including an honorary doctorate from Oxford University. His long-term plan had always been financial independence by the half-century mark, for these were unsettling times in Europe. Shortly after the *Joseph* premiere, Archduke Ferdinand was assassinated in Sarajevo; a month later Europe was plunged into world war. On the day of the assassination Strauss was in London for performances of *Josephslegende*, but an anti-German mood prevailed throughout the city and the London premiere was not well received. By 1 August, with the outbreak of World War I, Strauss's dream collapsed: thirty years' worth of savings, administered by British banker Edgar Speyer (*Salome*'s dedicatee), were confiscated by the British government; retirement was now out of the question. Strauss was in San Martino di Castrozza when war broke out and with difficulty had to make his way through Austrian troop transports over the Brenner pass.

Strauss the cosmopolitan nationalist presents us with conflicting views of his attitude toward the war. The man who, weeks before conflict broke out, received honors from Italy, France, and England, who kept his savings in British banks, wrote in his diary on 2 August 1914: "War and victory! Hail Germany! They won't make us back down!" On the last page of the completed short score to Act I of *Die Frau ohne Schatten*, Strauss wrote "[Completed] on the day of the victory of Saarburg. Hail to our brave army, hail to our great German fatherland." But as usual with Strauss, such statements, which have a curiously hollow ring to them, are difficult to take at face value. We know, indeed, that the apolitical, self-absorbed composer was equally annoyed with the First World War; not only had it robbed him of his life's savings, but threatened to conscript his delicate son into military service, despite Strauss's efforts to keep him out. Strauss, who had an aversion to military pomp and flashy displays of patriotism, could support the war only on the most abstract level. From outside, Strauss, the composer of the Kaiser's military marches, was viewed as a fervent German patriot, yet within Germany many questioned his lack of patriotic support. One year into the war he wrote to Hofmannsthal how "sickening" it was

> to read how Young Germany is to emerge cleansed and purified from this 'glorious' war, when in fact one must be thankful if the poor blighters are at least cleansed of their lice and bed-bugs and cured of their infections and once more weaned from murder![20]

Hofmannsthal was immediately conscripted into military service, which – much to the composer's annoyance – significantly delayed Act III of *Die Frau ohne Schatten*. Just two days before he wrote of "war and victory" Strauss declared that

> poets ought to be permitted to stay at Home. There is plenty of cannon fodder available: critics, stage producers who have their own ideas, actors who act Molière, etc. I am convinced that there will be no world war, that the little altercation with Serbia will soon be over, and that I will receive the third act of my *Frau ohne Schatten*. May the devil take the damned Serbs.[21]

Indeed, the period of gestation for *Die Frau ohne Schatten* was so long that it is hard to remember that it was originally to have followed *Der Rosenkavalier*; Strauss had intended to balance his "Comedy for Music" with a weightier subject. But *Ariadne*, the experimental "interim work," soon became a major preoccupation (and irritation) during the years following *Rosenkavalier*. In early 1914 Hofmannsthal returned to his metaphysical fairy tale, which incorporated elements of *Das steinerne Herz*, and Strauss began composing the opera later that year. *Die Frau ohne Schatten*, with its dense orchestration, rich polyphony, and intricate symbolism, is Strauss's longest and most complex stage work, yet in many ways – as we shall see – it is also his most personal.

Such a vast undertaking was difficult to launch, for it required extensive discussions, prodded no doubt by pragmatic questions of clarification from the composer. A private retreat was the answer, and the enterprising, often underestimated, Pauline suggested that he and Hofmannsthal take a working holiday, on which they could discuss the newly-completed scenario extensively, but at their leisure. Hofmannsthal, who usually preferred a physical distance from his collaborator, surprisingly agreed. This three-week chauffeured automobile tour of Italy (Verona, Bologna, and on down to Rome) marked the only time when composer and librettist spent more than a few days together and proved to be a marvelous experience for both men. In a letter to his father, Hofmannsthal described Strauss as one of the most pleasant traveling companions he had ever known.

Die Frau ohne Schatten is unique among Strauss's operas for its vast dimension, seriousness of purpose, and sustained depth of feeling. Despite their retreat, Hofmannsthal realized that before he could create verses destined for music, he would first have to write a prose version in order to work out the thematic and symbolic intricacies. Once things were clarified in the poet's mind, he was ready to send text to the composer, always knowing that Strauss required human situations, conflicts, and passions in order to compose; abstractions left him cold. When all is said and done, *Die Frau ohne Schatten* – despite its fairy-tale setting, magical transformations, singing unborn children – is an opera about the search for humanity, explored on multiple levels.

On the level of the upper world, the Empress "stands between two worlds," according to Hofmannsthal, "not released by one, not accepted by the other." The Empress, daughter of the omniscient, invisible Keikobad, has been captured by the Emperor while she was at first in the form of a gazelle. She has no human relationship with her husband, she is little more than a trophy, a sexual object:

> At first light he slips from her, when the stars appear he is there again. His nights are her day, his days are her night.

The world of the Empress, the immortal world, is one of constant bliss, but one lacking human passion. In order to attain mortality (to give and receive human love) she must accept the totality of the human condition: life's pain, death, and sacrifice. In short, in order to feel the fire of human passion, she must accept life's shadow, ultimately borne of light. Her heart is a stone, a crystal through which light merely passes.

Through all the complexities of the plot shone one fundamental theme, one that was dear to Strauss's heart well before he met Hofmannsthal: that of marriage, fidelity, and domestic love. This common theme created the strongest bond between composer and poet and sustained their relationship over decades. It is the very fidelity that Hofmannsthal spoke of in his so-called Ariadne letter of July 1911 (quoted above) when he was simultaneously drafting *Die Frau ohne Schatten*. And though the work's title suggests that the principal subject concerns the shadowless Empress's search for humanity, the subplot of the Dyer, his wife, and their troubled marriage touched Strauss more deeply than any other aspect of the story. His own marriage was troubled during this time, and Hofmannsthal hinted at this domestic friction when he suggested that the Dyer's wife could be modeled "in all discretion" after Pauline Strauss, whose outspoken, temperamental personality repelled the Austrian poet. Indeed, in a scenario draft not sent to the composer, Hofmannsthal wrote that it would not only incorporate elements of Mozart's *Magic Flute*, but the heart of the drama would revolve around "a bizarre figure like Strauss's wife."

Barak, the dyer, is easily the most sympathetic character in the opera and undeniably represents the composer himself. The Dyer's wife, who at first would give her shadow to the Empress, wants more than mere marriage to Barak, the cloth dyer. She wants an identity beyond her husband (unlike her husband, she has no name save being identified as his wife). In this sense, the comparison with Pauline rings true, for despite her early career she was increasingly known as the composer's wife. The intensity of her struggles with private and personal life is strongly felt in this score: the Act III duet of reconciliation between Barak and his wife ("Mir / dir anvertraut") is unquestionably the most moving passage in the entire opera.

In their different ways, the Empress and the Dyer's Wife learned something that Elektra could never know: that in order to attain humanity one must admit a responsibility to the past, present, and future of humanity. Elektra is obsessed by her past, has no present, and has only vague notions of a future. She is revolted as her sister, Chrysothemis, sings "Kinder will ich haben" (I want to have children). Hofmannsthal reminds us that "the individual can only remain to endure where a compromise has been struck between the community and the individual." He concluded that an individual of true humanity finds that connection, that thread linking past, present, and future and discovers that this very thread connects us to our civilization. At the end of Act I of *Die Frau ohne Schatten*, as the Dyer and his wife are sleeping separately, the Watchmen sing:

> Married folk under the roofs of this town,
> love one another more than your own lives,
> and recall: it is not for your own lives' sake
> that the seed of life is given to you,
> but for the sake of your love alone . . .
> you are the bridges spanning the chasm
> over which the dead find their way back to life!

Strauss once called his *Frau ohne Schatten* a "child of sorrow," and it was a child that did not enter the world without a lengthy, painful labor: from its inception in 1911 to its premiere in 1919, at the newly reorganized Vienna State Opera, where Strauss would serve as co-director with Franz Schalk. This work, with its rich symbolism and occasionally overwrought polyphony, stands as a compelling epitaph for post-Romanticism: it was conceived in peacetime, composed during conflict, and premiered to a lukewarm reception after the Treaty of Versailles. The end of World War One marked the end of the two most famous decades of Strauss's life, who at age fifty-four would have to start again. Not only had he lost his own hard-earned fortune in England but he also saw the political and economic collapse of the Wilhelmine era.

The loss of money meant the loss of artistic autonomy, but Strauss believed he had served Berlin faithfully enough, and had earned enough prestige that he could compensate for that loss with a flexible new contract that offered more time to compose. However, the Intendant of the Berlin Opera, Baron Georg von Hülsen – who had given in to Strauss on earlier occasions – had reached his limit and the composer was released in April 1918. Neither, of course, foresaw the political turmoil of the November Revolution; neither knew that in just seven months the German court, including its opera, would dissolve, leaving von Hülsen, but not Strauss, out of a job. Indeed, on the day of the 11 November armistice, Strauss was appointed interim artistic advisor, along with Leo Blech, to Georg Dröscher, interim director of the Berlin Opera. Though he worked hard to ensure the institution would survive the period of transition, Strauss was ready to leave Berlin after twenty years of service. On 25 November he submitted his official resignation and negotiations with Vienna were already underway. Strauss's old friend Max von Schillings was finally appointed as his successor in November 1919 and would become the first director of the reorganized, and renamed, Berlin State Opera.

Strauss left Berlin just when a new generation of composers (such as Kurt Weill and Paul Hindemith) were about to make their mark in the German capital, composers who embraced the new spirit of the Weimar Republic and rejected post-Romanticism as a dead legacy, an uncomfortable reminder of the Wilhelmine era. Though hardly one to be counted among this new group of composers, Strauss too was weary of post-Wagnerian music, even if he, himself, had helped define it. As early as summer 1916, before completing Act II of *Die Frau ohne Schatten*, Strauss had already begun to distance himself from Romanticism; he expressed an overriding wish to get away from myth, allegory, and the supernatural. What he desired more than anything was a fresh, modern subject. Letters to Hofmannsthal show a composer who resolved to shed himself of "Wagnerian musical armor," who declared that "*Die Frau ohne Schatten* will be the last Romantic opera," and who was determined to move in a new direction. The new path would lead Strauss from Berlin to Vienna, from *Die Frau ohne Schatten* to *Intermezzo*, from a metaphysical marriage opera to a domestic sex comedy. Only the protean Richard Strauss could explore such divergent worlds with such apparent ease.

4 Between two empires: Strauss in the 1920s

On the evening of 7 November 1918, Strauss conducted *Salome* in Berlin. At the time he had no idea that it would be the last work to be performed by the Court Opera, for the next day Kaiser Wilhelm fled to Holland, and within twenty-four hours a German republic was declared. On the day of this so-called Weimar proclamation, Strauss tersely noted in his calendar that he had waited an hour at the Berlin-Zoo station for a train to Munich that never arrived: "No train, abdication of the Kaiser, republic, revolution. Suitcase packed, one hour at the Zoo [station], evening playing skat with [Willi] Levin." It is irresistible, on one level, to interpret this curious entry as evidence of a shallow, self-possessed, card-playing composer who viewed the cataclysmic fall of the German Empire merely as a personal annoyance. But it would be equally facile to say – as some commentators have done – that in the wake of Germany's defeat Strauss woke up to a world he no longer understood. Such an assertion would ignore the resilience and resourcefulness of a composer who, though he may have had little sympathy for the aesthetics of *neue Sachlichkeit* or epic theater, was still well in tune with the world in which he lived. Where Sibelius and Elgar – composers of Strauss's generation – had felt an increasing sense of alienation in the years following the war (ultimately giving up composing), Strauss continued to write music up to the end of his life.

Amidst the turmoil and misery of 1918, cultural activity in Berlin moved at an unprecedented pace, and it was an explosion on all artistic fronts: music, theater, radio, the visual arts, and film. A host of new names appeared on the scene: Paul Hindemith, Kurt Weill, and Ernst Krenek in music; Erwin Piscator, Leopold Jessner, and Bertolt Brecht in theater; Otto Dix, George Grosz, and Max Beckmann in painting; and Robert Wiene, Paul Wegener, and Fritz Lang in film. Chaos may have signaled promise to some, but for others – such as Strauss – it was cause for pessimism, and, indeed, throughout November 1918, the composer confessed to moments of significant depression.

A despondent Strauss described the former Court Opera as a "madhouse," and during those early, critical months the institution was doubtless in a state of utter confusion. But the composer, who had brought the opera house to an unprecedented level of prestige during his twenty years in Berlin, was determined to help save it before leaving, and he was largely successful. His desire to move on to Vienna predated the chaos of November, and we recall that in April 1918, under the old regime of Georg von Hülsen, his Berlin contract had not been renewed. A warm relationship between Strauss and the Austrian capital had been growing for some years. The second version of *Ariadne* premiered there in 1916, and Vienna celebrated its first ever Strauss festival two years later: the very month of his dismissal in Berlin.

The post-war situation in Viennese cultural life was hardly ideal, but not as traumatic as in the German capital. The desperate Emperor Karl, whose two-year reign marked a sad end to the 600-year Habsburg dynasty, agreed to renounce all monarchical control over the government on 11 November; with that renunciation (and the ensuing breakup of the Austro-Hungarian Empire) Vienna went from imperial capital to the seat of a small new republic. Karl's last Intendant at the Court Opera, Leopold von Andrian, had already been making overtures to Strauss to become its new director by late summer 1918.

The previous director, Hans Gregor, was not himself a musician, but rather an expert administrator who brought gifted singers and great reputation to the Vienna Opera during his seven-year stint, which ended in 1918. Franz Schalk, a student of Anton Bruckner and conductor at the opera since the days of Mahler, was made interim director until fall 1919. Hofmannsthal was, at first, not convinced that Strauss's southward move was in the best interest of the newly restructured and renamed State Opera. He feared that, rather than rebuild the institution, the composer would make it a venue for his own works, and in August 1918 he voiced his doubts directly to Strauss:

> The great danger of your life, to which you surrender and from which you try to escape in almost periodic cycles, is a neglect of all the higher standards of intellectual existence. Any attempt to place oneself above ideas and institutions is an utter negation of what matters to civilized human beings and, insofar as your works themselves form part of what matters in intellectual life, it is they, however much you mean to foster them, which will have to pay the eventual penalty. But I do not think that you have reached the point at which you can understand the connection.[1]

This instance was neither the first nor the last time that Hofmannsthal would underestimate his collaborator, particularly the depth of his musical and creative abilities. Strauss, undeterred by his librettist's skepticism, knew that he could balance self interest with the needs of the institution; he also knew that at this critical moment in Austrian history the newly reformed opera house could benefit from the weight of his artistic presence. Hofmannsthal, who later reversed his opinion, was hardly alone in his fears, for no sooner had an agreement been reached in April 1919 than staff members of Vienna Opera lodged a formal protest against the appointment, a protest likely orchestrated in part by Strauss's rival, Felix Weingartner, who himself had eyes on the State Opera post. They argued that Strauss's initial agreement had been made under the auspices of the monarchy, that his yearly salary of 80,000 kronen (plus 1,200 kronen per performance) was too high in view of the shaky post-war economy, and that his loyalty to Vienna would be compromised by his ties to Berlin.

The first two assertions were undoubtedly true, but the fact that Strauss's Vienna commitment amounted to only five months a year had nothing to do with a desire to maintain simultaneous artistic control in Berlin; rather, it allowed him the necessary time for his creative work and guest conducting. As a man approaching sixty Strauss well knew the burdens of balancing conducting and composing; moreover, he had seen what a ten-month-a-year conducting contract had done to Mahler when he was at the Court Opera. The composer remained peacefully in Garmisch amidst the turmoil that was capped by a telegram (11 April 1919) – signed by such Viennese luminaries as Hofmannsthal, Stefan Zweig, Paul Stefan, Alma Mahler, Adolf Loos, Arthur Schnitzler, and Alfred Roller – urging him to ignore the protests and come to Vienna. Franz Schalk's endorsement, two days later, ensured that the appointment would indeed go through. In fact, a month later Strauss arrived at the Austrian capital to take part in a celebration marking the fiftieth anniversary of the Vienna Opera House on the Ringstrasse, which had opened in 1869. There he conducted *Die Zauberflöte, Fidelio, Tristan, Der Rosenkavalier,* and *Ariadne auf Naxos.*

The contractual arrangement could hardly have been better for Strauss, who demanded not only a high salary and essentially a January-through-May work schedule but a co-directorship with Franz Schalk in which the composer was blatantly (though unofficially) the "greater equal" of the pair. The fact that the division of duties was never clearly articulated led to friction within the first year and to Strauss's ultimate resignation within a few years. But the reality was that Schalk took care of the everyday running of the institution while Strauss made the broader artistic decisions, something Schalk had enjoyed doing under the previous directorship of Hans Gregor. Schalk put the best face on a situation he inwardly resented; he had worked his way upward through the ranks, and now an outsider – and a German at that – had come to town to tell him how to program operas for the venerable Austrian institution.

Strauss undeniably took advantage of his artistic position in the programming of his own works – the same had been true to a lesser extent in Berlin – but he also brought the Viennese Opera to remarkable heights. In the August 1918 letter to Strauss, Hofmannsthal had voiced concern that the Wagner and Mozart repertoires might suffer with the composer as artistic director in Vienna, but these were the very repertoires to which Strauss brought new vigor. He featured a new production of *Lohengrin* for his Wagner debut (Mahler had done the same for his Wagner debut in 1897), and it was soon followed by a remarkable Ring cycle. The Mozart repertoire achieved unprecedented stature in Vienna with highly acclaimed productions of *Don Giovanni*, *Così fan tutte*, and *Le Nozze di Figaro*, and – with the collaboration of Max Reinhardt, Schalk, and Hofmannsthal – Strauss would help create the Salzburg Festival, which opened in 1920. On another front, Strauss increased the number of new operas to be performed at the State Opera, something that the more conservative Schalk had always resisted. The Strauss years saw operas by Hans Pfitzner, Franz Schreker, Julius Bittner, Erich Korngold, and Franz Schmidt among others.

The many artistic successes were all the more remarkable given the dismal financial state of the opera house management and the Austrian economy in general. Most European currency was unstable, the dollar being the economic standard of the day, and, for that reason, the Vienna Philharmonic went on tour to South America in their search for hard currency. Strauss, Schalk, and the orchestra embarked on a trip that began in August and ended some three months later. Most of the time was spent in Rio de Janeiro and Buenos Aires, where the Vienna Philharmonic played a host of concerts in a grueling schedule that gave Strauss little opportunity for composing except while aboard ship. This, of course, was not Strauss's original plan, for the off months were to have been for creative work and limited guest conducting. Yet with increasing economic insecurity the composer, still smarting from the financial losses of World War I, became increasingly concerned about the need for hard currency,

14   The opera house on the Vienna Ringstrasse, where Strauss served as
     co-director from 1919 to 1924

and, indeed, he scheduled another tour – to the United States – for the
following season.

In a remarkably matter-of-fact tone, Strauss informed Schalk that he
would be leaving for the United States in October 1921 and would not
return until mid-January; moreover, he would be taking with him some
of Vienna's best singers: Elisabeth Schumann and possibly Maria
Jeritza, Richard Schubert, and Maria Ivogün. Schalk was dumbfounded:

> What in the world attracts you [to America]? When you are not here
> doing your appointed cultural work of a higher order, I can only think
> it is because you don't wish your composing to be disturbed; but to
> show the Americans how to make music – don't take it wrong – I
> don't understand it. And don't be angry with me if I show my
> incomprehension so openly. I had always thought that your mission,
> whether in the productive or reproductive arts, was at the highest
> level, in the best imaginable milieu.[2]

Strauss shot back:

> How nice of you to miss me so dearly, and you ask me why I am going
> to America? Not for my enjoyment! After England seized my major

savings, I have no reason to expect a pension from any quarter – I am solely dependent on the royalties from works if something should stop me from conducting. Operatic successes are mutable; if my royalties ever dry up, which I hope will not happen for yet a while, I will be a beggar and leave my family in "poverty and scandal." I must free myself of this worry before I can ever work in peace again.[3]

Poverty and scandal were not idle, abstract expressions for Strauss, whose father, we recall, was born in poverty and illegitimacy, working his way into the middle class only by virtue of his musical talent and fierce tenacity. Richard was obsessed with the notion of financial independence not only for the sake of peace and privacy but so that he could provide financial security for his family after his death.

But Strauss was also determined to raise money, through some benefit concerts, for the Vienna Opera and Salzburg Festival while in America, and he managed to bring back the tidy sum of $13,000. Moreover, Strauss agreed not to take Vienna's top singers with him, and in the end he toured only with Elisabeth Schumann, for whom he had already orchestrated a number of his early songs for symphony concert purposes. His whirlwind tour, which included ten concerts and thirty song recitals, took him to New York, Boston, Wheeling (West Virginia), St. Louis, Kansas City, Indianapolis, Detroit, Madison, Milwaukee, Cincinnati, Chicago, and Reading (Pennsylvania).

Strauss became acquainted with Schumann in 1917 and was so impressed with her voice that he brought her to the Vienna State Opera. She may well have been part of the reason that the composer returned to lieder composition after a hiatus of more than a decade. Most of Strauss's songs were composed before the turn of the century, and many believed that after his wife Pauline had retired from singing in 1906, Strauss had given up composing songs. Against the backdrop of postwar unrest, the lied – with its rich German-Romantic tradition – had become somewhat anachronistic, yet these later songs differ significantly from many of those composed in his early period. Among his works from 1918 was a collection of songs very much in the cynical spirit of the time: *Krämerspiegel*, the composer's only real song cycle. These biting, sarcastic texts were written for Strauss by Alfred

15 Strauss and Franz Schalk: co-directors of the Vienna State Opera (1919–1924)

Kerr, taking deadly aim at the music publishing industry. The publishing house Bote und Bock had threatened to sue Strauss for not giving them the dozen songs that had been promised by contract, to which he responded by sending them these venomous works, which were promptly returned without comment. And given the stinging puns in such songs as "Einst kam der Bock als Bote," it is easy to see why:

> Einst kam der Bock als Bote
> Zum Rosenkavalier ans Haus;
> Er klopft mit seiner Pfote,
> Den Eingang wehrt ein Rosenstrauss
>
> [Once a goat came as a messenger
> To the house of the Rose Cavalier;
> He knocked with his hoof,
> The entrance was guarded by a rose bouquet]

The eighth song stands out among these obscure pieces be
the opening theme was later used to introduce the final s
Capriccio (1941), and, indeed, it may well be the most beautif
he ever composed – all the more remarkable given that it v
not by love or beauty but rather by spiteful anger. The s
the long, lyrical piano introduction (in a song-withov
is its negation by the harsh, dissonant vocal part
with the lines:

> Art is threatened by merchants
> And there you have it.
> They bring Death to music
> And Transfiguration to themselves.[4]

Here we confront another expressi
composer who sailed to America
tation, who once played in War
the incompatibility of music and

During this time Strauss was intere
Op. 68 lieder, dedicated to Elisabeth Sc
Clemens Brentano, Op. 67 includes three song
Shakespeare's *Hamlet* and three songs from Goethe
Divan, and Op. 69 contains settings of Achim von Arnim and
Heine. These songs, with their frequent coloratura, reflect his expe
ence as opera composer, and the operatic connection is even more evi-
dent in the composition of the Op. 71 *Drei Hymnen* for voice and
orchestra. These three songs, setting texts by Friedrich Hölderlin,
mark the high point of his return to the genre after World War I,
though he referred to his orchestral songs not as lieder but rather as
Gesänge or, in this case, *Hymnen*. The early nineteenth-century poet
Hölderlin had been rediscovered by the young Nietzsche, who derived
much of his early thought from his poetry in the years surrounding the
Birth of Tragedy. Hölderlin's work, with its focus on love and the godly
that dwells in nature and the human mind, no doubt rekindled
the Nietzschean spirit that created *Also sprach Zarathustra* and the

NOTES/TO DO

Alpensinfonie. The Op. 71 songs were Strauss's first compositions from Vienna, and they were premiered in Berlin, while Strauss was on his American tour.

The composer's letters to Pauline, who stayed behind, suggest that despite all the concerts, receptions, parties, and tributes the composer was in a gloomy state. On the one hand, he was trying to generate capital for his future independence, but on the other, he knew all too well how much precious time he had to sacrifice. "When do I finally get to enjoy my own life?" a despondent Strauss asked Pauline from Philadelphia. For him enjoyment could mean only two things: composing and being with his family; the extensive touring allowed neither. Indeed, beyond the songs, the composer had been able to write precious little since the premiere of *Die Frau ohne Schatten*, which, though it was first performed in 1919, was completed in 1918. Four years later, he had only composed songs, though he was putting the final touches, while aboard ship, on a harmless, escapist ballet recalling a bygone Vienna, a remarkable miscalculation that only worsened Strauss's state of mind.

Schlagobers, the Viennese term for whipped cream, was never intended to be anything more than simple ballet, a work "for the feet of ballerinas, not for the heads of philosophers," as one contemporary critic put it. A cross, of sorts, between Tschaikovsky's *Nutcracker* and Ravel's *L'Enfant et les Sortilèges*, Strauss's ballet (text by the composer) involves a boy who, following the old custom of a trip to the sweet shop after first confirmation, becomes sick from overindulging and later has a dream in which the various sweets come to life. Composed in 1922, during a time of hyper-inflation, when a hard roll could sometimes constitute the evening meal, dancing pralines and pastries left a bad taste in many mouths, and the work was soon dubbed a "millionaire's ballet"; it failed in the very city to whom it was dedicated. The premiere itself had to be delayed until 1924 because of rising production costs and a depleted opera budget. Without the help of Hofmannsthal, Strauss could only offer a period piece, à la *Rosenkavalier*, but without its complexity or psychological depth. Strauss took the setback particularly hard:

People always expect ideas from me, big things. Haven't I the right,
after all, to write what music I please? I cannot bear the tragedy of the
present time. I want to create joy. I need it.[5]

Strauss realized his mistake, and though he made an orchestral-suite
arrangement, he never seriously promoted the work beyond its earliest performances. As misguided as *Schlagobers* seemed, with its rejection of anything complex or problematic, Strauss's turn away from the
myth and metaphysics of *Die Frau ohne Schatten* suggests a composer
weary of post-Romanticism, and indeed before completing the score
to *Die Frau*, he had asked Hofmannsthal for "a fine, happy idea that will
definitely help me out on the new road."

While *Schlagobers* was a detour off this new road, Strauss continued with *Intermezzo* (1923), his major work of the period, an operatic
project that had preoccupied him for a number of years. As early as
1911, Strauss had expressed interest in composing a modern
comedy some time in the future, and his interest resurfaced in May
1916:

> As for a new opera, I have two things in mind: either an entirely
> modern, absolutely realistic domestic and character comedy of the
> kind I have outlined to you before, when you referred me to
> [Hermann] Bahr – or some amusing piece of love and intrigue.[6]

Hofmannsthal was appalled, especially by the second suggestion
which was to involve a female spy as principal character, the wife of an
ambassador who, for the sake of love, betrays her country. "You'll say
trash!" Strauss wrote, "But then we musicians are known for our poor
taste in aesthetic matters, and besides, if you were to do a thing like
that it wouldn't be trash." Hofmannsthal could barely conceal his
amazement:

> I could not help having a good laugh over your letter. The things you
> propose to me are to my taste truly horrid and might put one off
> becoming a librettist for the rest of one's life – I mean put off not just
> anyone, but me personally.[7]

Strauss probably realized that the latter idea bordered on kitsch, but he was determined to move forward with his domestic comedy, a desire that was partly inspired by his delight in composing the comic *Vorspiel* (with its down-to-earth humor and finely nuanced interplay between speech, recitative, and aria) for the revised *Ariadne* of 1916. Taking Hofmannsthal's advice, he solicited the help of Bahr, whom the composer had known since the time of the *Elektra* premiere in 1909. Bahr had written an extensive, laudatory review of the opera, and his future wife, Anna Mildenburg, had sung Klytämnestra for the later Viennese premiere; she remained Strauss's favorite interpreter of the role. The year of the *Elektra* premiere Hermann Bahr published a domestic comedy of his own (*Das Konzert*), which he dedicated to Strauss, who may well have served as a model for the leading male role – a successful musician who is frequently on tour, leaving his wife at home. The Strauss dedication could not have been more appropriate, for the play touched upon so many of the themes that had been preoccupying Strauss since the turn of the century: the state of marriage in the modern world, communication between the sexes, the question of fidelity and marriage.

Strauss decided that his comedy, which he called a *Spieloper*, would be based on an actual event in his domestic life, an event that took place around the time he devised the program for his *Symphonia domestica* (1904). Two decades later, Strauss's *opera domestica* revisited the time when his wife threatened to divorce him, an act based on a case of mistaken identity (discussed in Chapter 3).

It is not difficult to imagine how awkward Bahr must have felt writing a text based on such an emotional, personal event in the composer's private life. His solution was to tone down the autobiographical aspects, where possible, much to the frustration of Strauss, who wanted quite the opposite. Beyond matters of characterization the composer was also dissatisfied with the dramatic flow, which he believed relied too much on self-contained – sometimes overwrought – scenes. Strauss wanted more space for music with scenes and characters more sketchlike, "almost just cinematic scenes" where the music says everything, the text providing some pace-setting catchwords. Bahr, who ultimately confessed that he simply could not visualize the characters in the same manner as Strauss, remained unable to satisfy the composer's demands, and the playwright suggested that he write the libretto himself.

Given Strauss's insecurities as a librettist (he had produced his own libretto to the failed *Guntram*), Bahr's encouragement for the composer to go it alone was just the boost that he needed, and he threw himself into the project with an enthusiasm not shown since *Der Rosenkavalier*. Above everything else, Strauss believed he was creating a new operatic genre, one that reflected modern Weimar Germany. So novel was the work that the composer, for the first time, felt compelled to write a preface to the score, a preface that offered insights on singing and acting based on Strauss's experiences as an opera conductor. He discusses wide-ranging vocal styles (spoken dialogue, secco recitative, accompanied recitative, aria) from Mozart to Wagner and how, through an intricate and often rapid interplay of these styles, realism of expression can be achieved.

Unlike *Schlagobers*, *Intermezzo* was very much a work of its time, and on a general level the artistic aims seem consonant with those of Gustav Hartlaub, who coined the term *neue Sachlichkeit* (new objectivity) in 1923:

> [*Neue Sachlichkeit*] expresses itself in the enthusiasm for the
> immediate reality as a result of the desire to take things entirely
> objectively on a material basis without immediately investing them
> with ideal implications.[8]

This new aesthetic flourished in German cultural life of the 1920s. One important musical incarnation of *neue Sachlichkeit* was the *Zeitoper* (topical opera), a work for the stage that emphasized *Alltäglichkeit*, focusing on the realistic world of the everyday. This genre did not emerge until the late 1920s, but it was clearly foreshadowed by *Intermezzo*, the first major German opera of the post-war era.

Though *Die Frau ohne Schatten* and *Intermezzo* are based on the theme of marriage, and though the composer's wife served as a model for both female leads, the two operas could not aesthetically be further apart: one opera opens in the spirit world of the invisible, omniscient Keikobad, while the other thrusts its audience, as voyeurs, into the middle of domestic bickering. Christine (alias Pauline) well exemplifies the manifold types of vocal expression outlined in Strauss's preface: she speaks when talking on the phone, giving orders to the servants, or reads aloud from the newspaper; she sings in dry recitative when undertaking business matters; arioso is for her conversations with a handsome young baron who flirts with her because she has money. Christine sings only rarely in a lyrical style, as she sinks in reverie by the fire, bids her son goodnight, and is reconciled with her husband at the end in a duet.

Intermezzo was the first Strauss opera to premiere in Dresden since Der Rosenkavalier, and those who expected a continuation of that tradition were surprised by this unprecedented new work, in which most of the lyrical moments were given to the orchestra in the form of symphonic interludes. Many were also surprised by the intentional cinematic qualities of the numerous short, open-ended scenes that segued or dissolved into orchestral interludes. Film was the most important new artistic genre in Weimar Germany; by the end of the 1920s Germany produced more films than the rest of Europe combined. The cinema changed the way people thought about live theater, and many plays and even some operas not only used cinematic techniques but actually incorporated film projection into the production, such as Kurt Weill's Royal Palace (1927) and Alan Berg's Lulu (1935). Though it is tempting to see Strauss's modern domestic comedy as a kind of response to a new era in German culture, his original ideas date back to 1916.

Reactions to Intermezzo were overwhelmingly positive, many critics expressing a sense of relief, given the mixed results of Josephslegende, Die Frau ohne Schatten, and Schlagobers. Reviews contained terms that would become regularly associated with the Zeitopern of the later 1920s: "Alltagsprosa," "Milieuechtheit," and "nüchterne Sachlichkeit." One critic suggested that the work should be thought of not as an "intermezzo," but rather as an "overture to a new era of German opera." Even Paul Stefan, writing for the progressive *Musikblätter des Anbruch*, and Arnold Schoenberg were impressed. Schoenberg, indeed, felt almost embarrassed to admit that he liked the work and offered condescending praise in a letter to his former student, Anton Webern:

> I have recently heard *Intermezzo* by Strauss and must say, to my greatest surprise, that it was not at all unlikeable. I find it inconceivable that he can play comedy and make himself appear better than he is . . . And since this presentation leaves me with the definite impression that one is dealing with a very genial, warm person – a consequence not of his art, but of his personality – it convincingly reveals a side of his personality that has actually captivated me.[9]

Strauss had ended his *Intermezzo* preface by stating, almost apologetically that

> By turning its back upon the popular love-and-murder interests of the usual opera libretto, and by taking its subject matter perhaps too exclusively from real life, this new work blazes a path for musical and dramatic composition which others after me may perhaps negotiate with more talent and better fortune.

The new work did blaze a path of sorts, leading to such later *Zeitopern* as Hindemith's *Neues vom Tage* and Schoenberg's *Von heute auf morgen*.

The original plan, dating back to 1919, was that *Intermezzo* would be premiered in Vienna; Strauss, who generally remained silent about the progress of his work, kept Schalk informed on a fairly regular basis. Things ran smoothly until February 1924, when the issue of government funding of the premiere came into question, and Strauss – weary from negotiating funds for the *Schlagobers* premiere – finally chose Dresden. By then the working relationship between Strauss and Schalk had seriously deteriorated, and, in truth, the co-directorship was a plan doomed from the start: Schalk felt he had earned seniority through years of loyal work, whereas Strauss thought he deserved it for artistic reasons; Schalk, the Austrian, believed he knew Viennese tastes better than a German, while Strauss considered Schalk's tastes narrow and provincial. The main problem, however, was that Schalk worked the full season, while Strauss worked only five months a year, though he wanted authority over all final artistic decisions. In an age where most long-distance negotiating was done by mail, Schalk resented undertaking the daily administration while Strauss basked in the international spotlight. It became increasingly difficult to conduct business in Vienna with the composer in Garmisch or on tour.

Schalk was not the only one annoyed by this arrangement. Julius Korngold, successor to Eduard Hanslick at the *Neue freie Presse* (and father of the Wunderkind composer), admired Strauss the composer, but had opposed his appointment from the start. He complained openly that Strauss's self-interest was detrimental to the institution, that he would borrow Vienna Opera singers for important Strauss performances in other cities, often leaving Schalk with vocalists of the second rank. Moreover, he viewed the composer as a spendthrift during a time of economic austerity. Other journalists and musical personalities joined in, including Weingartner, and an anti-Strauss faction soon wielded significant influence. The composer underestimated Schalk's power, and, when his contract was renewed in April 1924, he tried to make the removal of Schalk part of the agreement. While in Dresden rehearsing *Intermezzo* in late October, Strauss was informed that, to the contrary, Schalk's contract had just been renewed, and, further, he stipulated that in the composer's absence, he would assume full responsibility for artistic decisions. Strauss resigned immediately.

Not all critics were glad that Strauss was leaving. Heinrich Kralik, for example, accused the opera administration of caving in to mediocrity and likened the forced resignation to Mahler's dismissal decades earlier:

> Geniuses are hard to find. But we are in the fortunate position of having one. And are we going let him go? On account of opera

politics of the lowest level? For once, the "higher ups" should listen less to the advice of bureaucrats, diplomats, and other irresponsible advisors and more to the voice of the people, whose enthusiasm, love, and fidelity is manifested overwhelmingly whenever Richard Strauss appears on the podium.[10]

This incident blemished a year of supposed celebration, in which honors poured in for the composer's sixtieth birthday. He received honorary Viennese citizenship, and Strauss festivals were held in Berlin, Breslau, Dresden, Munich, and other European cities. And there was yet another cause for celebration in 1924, for Strauss's only child, Franz, married Alice von Grab, the daughter of Emanuel von Grab, a wealthy Prague industrialist with strong musical interests and connections. Strauss had known her father since 1907 when they were introduced in Prague by their mutual friend Leo Blech, the Berlin conductor. The composer, who had no daughter, developed – over time – a close relationship with Alice, who acted as his secretary and helped organize his manuscripts, letters, and other documents into what would become the Strauss Archive. The fact that Alice was Jewish, however, would create unforeseen problems for the Strauss family a decade later.

The composer's sixtieth year also saw the completion of a villa in Vienna, along the eastern edge of the Belvedere. The plot for the building, which was formerly the private garden of Archduke Franz Ferdinand, was given to Strauss on loan for sixty years by the city in exchange for the autograph score to Der Rosenkavalier and Schlagobers (later, Die ägyptische Helena), as well as his promise to conduct 100 performances over a period of five years for no fee. The mansion itself was built at his own expense with funds from his American tour and the financial support of his daughter-in-law's father.

Strauss's birthday milestone was a time not only for tribute but also for reappraisal. Critics and commentators such as Ernest Newman, Lazare Saminsky, and Theodor Adorno used the anniversary to write the composer's musical obituary, to proclaim his talent played out, and to declare his future moribund. Adorno's critique, which appeared in the Neue Zeitschrift für Musik, was particularly damning and lasting, remaining an unfortunate model for opinion for decades to come. This first full-length musical essay by the 21-year-old Adorno was a critique rooted in the high-modernist concept of the ideology of style, where a fundamental emphasis was placed on "value" in a musical work. "Value" was, in turn, defined by the notion of technical progress, by what Adorno called – in his inevitably Hegelian way – the "tendency of the materials." Style was thus a matter not of choice but of historical obligation, and art was not necessarily a question of pleasure or beauty but "the unfolding of truth" – a truth defined, of course, by Adorno himself.

According to this one-sided historical narrative Strauss had ostensibly become untrue to the materials of his age by the 1920s, ignoring the "demands of history," composing in an invalid tonal style that had long since been exhausted. The essence of the 1924 critique, which Adorno updated forty years later, was that in Strauss's music, form was little more than appearance; his work lacked objectivity (which is here understood to mean an authentic relationship with its society) and, ultimately, artistic truth – the very truth demanded by a new generation of modernists born in the 1870s and 80s. In his dialectical way, Adorno asserted that for art to be truthful, it must first confess its fictitiousness. As dated and reductive as this argument now seems, it was taken so seriously that it continued to permeate Strauss criticism well after the composer's death.

Adorno's essay was neither the first nor the last attack on the composer's music, but the sixty-year-old Strauss remained unfazed. He was also relieved to be out of the business of opera administration. The Schalk episode notwithstanding, his love for Vienna and her culture remained steadfast, and he enjoyed his role as regular guest conductor at the Vienna Opera and the concerts with the Vienna Philharmonic. Indeed, his very next project would be a tribute of sorts to Vienna with the making of a film version of Der Rosenkavalier, for which he provided the musical score, Hofmannsthal devised the screenplay, and the celebrated Robert Wiene served as director.

The film project, which was the idea of Hofmannsthal, can obviously be seen on one level as an exploitation of the opera's great success. The 1920s saw German cinema come into its own; it was the new theatrical medium, offering a host of possibilities. Opera directors, with their shrunken budgets, feared that this new, inexpensive form of entertainment might make opera obsolete. Moreover, would it irrevocably change audience expectations for operas of the future? Hofmannsthal unquestionably saw a lucrative opportunity, but he also saw an important artistic one as well. We recall Hofmannsthal's language crisis at the turn of the century, when he turned his back on lyric poetry and embraced the gestural world of theater. Language was indirect, general, impure, the product of consensus, but gesture was direct, undiluted, "a pure thought," according to Hofmannsthal. Thus, film (which was, of course, "silent" in 1925) was a genre that, even more than drama, relied on gesture, on pantomime, for its expression.

Both poet and composer were determined that the project would not be merely a film version of the opera. The libretto was therefore entirely recast into a two-act screenplay, and Strauss even included some new music. Though skeptical at first, he became more interested as the project unfolded, for he was a composer who was always preoccupied with the relationship between the musical and the visual. He was an avid museum visitor and, indeed, around the time of *Elektra*, he sketched out a symphonic work based on paintings in London's National Gallery. Strauss conducted the premiere not in a movie theater, but at the Dresden opera in January 1926; three months later, he went to London to conduct it at the Tivoli Cinema, never conducting it again.

While in Vienna Strauss befriended the Wittgenstein family. Paul, the older brother of Ludwig (the distinguished Viennese philosopher), asked Strauss, in 1919, to compose a piano concerto, a genre he had not explored since the *Burleske* of 1886. Paul Wittgenstein was a pianist of international renown, who had lost his right arm during World War I and commissioned a number of distinguished composers to write works for the left hand only. The best-known pieces are by

Ravel and Prokofiev, but he also engaged the talents of Benjamin Britten, Korngold, Franz Schmidt, and of course Strauss – the only composer to write a second commission for Wittgenstein.

When first asked, Strauss was reluctant to compose a concerto, to return to abstract instrumental composition. As Strauss got older he found he could compose only by connecting musical ideas with extra-musical phenomena: a libretto, a poem, or a program. The extra-musical spark that reversed his decision was a recent serious, life-threatening event in the family. His son Franz had contracted typhus while on his honeymoon in Egypt and remained in grave condition for some time. It was a terrible blow for the composer, who had just gained a daughter-in-law and now feared he might lose a son. In celebration of his son's recovery, Strauss composed a concerto for piano left hand and orchestra based on Franz's theme from *Symphonia domestica* – a theme that could not be quoted beyond three bars; the copyright was held by Bote und Bock, the very publishing house he had scorned in his *Krämerspiegel*.

He called the work a *Parergon*, a companion piece to *Symphonia domestica*, although the work lacks the warmth and joy of the symphonic poem. This score, in fact, contains some of the darkest, most turbulent music composed since *Elektra*, a direct result of the composer's bleak, anxious state of mind. Wittgenstein was delighted and commissioned yet another work, which Strauss called *Panathenäenzug* (1927) with the subtitle, "Symphonic Studies in the form of a Passacaglia." The overall form is that of an introduction, eighteen continuous variations over a repeated bass pattern, and a finale. The title, *Panathenäenzug* (Panathenian procession) refers to the annual festival of ancient Athens celebrating the birth of Athena. Every fourth year the festival culminated in a lavish procession, as immortalized in the Parthenon frieze. The inspiration for this second commission no doubt came from a 1924 ballet collaboration with Hofmannsthal, a reworking of Beethoven's *Ruins of Athens* ("Festive Spectacle with Dances and Choruses"), which itself includes a stylized Panathenian procession.

Compared with *Ariadne* or *Die Frau ohne Schatten*, the Beethoven project was admittedly a minor effort of the famous collaborators; the same can be said of their *Rosenkavalier* film project. Strauss was now well established in Vienna, but he had done nothing of significance with his Viennese collaborator since his arrival in the Austrian capital. Though the hiatus of activity could be explained by a host of valid reasons (transatlantic tours, work on *Intermezzo*), the fact remains that the relationship between Strauss and his librettist had reached an all-time low, and for reasons that are not hard to surmise. Hofmannsthal had always enjoyed working with Strauss from a distance; he made no secret of the fact that they had little in common beyond their mutual work. His initial plea for Strauss not to come to Vienna was primarily for the sake of the Opera, but surely a deeper anxiety stemmed from the proximity to Hofmannsthal's house in Rodaun, in the outskirts of Vienna.

In the Austrian capital the artistic relationship threatened to take on an awkward social dimension: "Of course our relationship is less easy," Hofmannsthal explained to Strauss, "for the very reason that it was once something so very special and rich in content."[11] Though he admired Strauss the artist, Hofmannsthal found it difficult to endure Strauss the man, and regular personal contact only brought to the surface those negative feelings that had been possible to ignore at a safe distance. Hofmannsthal saw in Strauss a certain coarseness, arrogance, and lack of artistic taste. But there was an inevitable cultural dimension as well, one difficult to separate from the personality. Strauss was German, a culture for which Hofmannsthal (and Franz Schalk, for that matter) had little sympathy. Strauss's letters to Hofmannsthal suggest a composer who did not fully understand his collaborator's inability to create at a moment's notice, his moody temperament, and – above all – his need for privacy. Or was this an act on Strauss's part, a way of getting the most out of Hofmannsthal that he possibly could? Whatever the case, Strauss was disappointed to discover that his move to Vienna did not mean that he and his collaborator would see each any more regularly, and he expressed his chagrin to Hofmannsthal on various occasions.

But after *Intermezzo*, the composer – now free of administrative duties at the opera – was determined to return to a major project with Hofmannsthal, something blithe and comic, approaching operetta. His desire for a Hofmannsthal comedy dates back to 1916, while in the midst of the weighty *Die Frau ohne Schatten*. Weary of the heavy, Wagnerian leitmotivic apparatus of *Die Frau*, Strauss – thinking back to the happy days of *Der Rosenkavalier* – believed comedy to be his strong suit for the next decade. It offered him a distance from the musical mechanics of Wagner; somewhat facetiously, he even declared his desire to become the Offenbach of the twentieth century. Hofmannsthal, in 1920, was delighted to lure the composer away from Wagnerian "erotic screaming," and he offered Strauss a light-hearted scenario, a mythological parody based on the story of Danae. But this was a time when their relationship was at its nadir and when Strauss had become increasingly preoccupied with *Intermezzo*; the Danae plan was soon forgotten.

Intermezzo had been a success in 1924 – even Hofmannsthal confessed to liking it – and it reinvigorated the composer's desire to compose more musical comedies. In the early months of 1922, Hofmannsthal devised yet another plan for mythological parody, one with direct connections to Offenbach, namely an operetta based on the story of Helen of Troy. Though it was shelved for a time, Strauss was ready for something new after his return from his South American tour of 1923. He had finished scoring *Intermezzo* while aboard ship and hoped to find a *Helena* scenario waiting for him upon his arrival in Garmisch: "preferably with entertaining ballet interludes; delightful elf or spirit choruses would also be most welcome ... Something delicate, amusing, warm-hearted!"

The poet was happy to oblige but warned Strauss that he must keep his end of the bargain, a more delicate musical style that was "easy-flowing," a lighter orchestra with none of the dense leitmotivic armor that had weighed down *Die Frau ohne Schatten*. The focus should be on the voices, and indeed from the earliest scenario Hofmannsthal had specific singers in mind: Maria Jeritza, Richard Tauber, Alfred Jerger.

Die ägyptische Helena never became an operetta, but it was their first and only *bel canto* work of sorts. Today, Helen remains one of Strauss's flashiest soprano roles. But the opera, especially in its more complex, symbolic second act, proved to be a work somewhat removed from the delicate, lighter world of *la belle Helène*, for Hofmannsthal could never bring himself to write something entirely frivolous. Nevertheless, there are delightful satirical touches in Act I: an omniscient singing shell and mischievous elves. Helen of Troy has been unfaithful to her husband Menelaus, who wishes to kill her. After a storm at sea they arrive at the palace of Aithra, who secretly gives Menelaus a draft of lotus juice, causing amnesia. She convinces him that Paris had abducted a phantom Helen; the real one – who remained faithful – has waited for him in Aithra's palace. Act II begins in their bedroom, during their "second wedding night," which offers Strauss the opportunity for Helen's grandiose aria ("Zweite Brautnacht"), the most famous passage in the opera.

Hofmannsthal, who often chided Strauss for becoming bogged down during the creative process, himself leaves the lighter world of satire while writing Act II, when things take a more profound turn. With the second curtain Hofmannsthal brings into focus themes central to his other libretti: memory, fidelity, the restoration of trust. As much as she would like to, Helen cannot live with her husband if he remains under the spell of amnesia, even though she knows full well that he may kill her if the spell is broken. Where Ariadne had given herself to death and was thereby transformed, here Helen likewise offers herself to death (risking her life by offering her husband the potion of remembrance) and is similarly transfigured. And in turn she transforms her husband, for the jealous Menelaus is finally able to resolve the good and bad in Helen (and himself) and – reborn – he accepts her: "Ever the same, ever new."

Strauss, around the time of his *Symphonia domestica*, remarked that "marriage is the most profound event in life." Indeed, his preoccupation with domestic relationships, with marriage and fidelity, formed a continuous theme throughout his life's work and a common bond

16   Portrait of Strauss (1925) by Ferdinand Schmutzer during the composer's
     Vienna period

between composer and librettist. With Die ägyptische Helena Strauss's
trilogy of marriage operas was now complete. Die Frau ohne Schatten
began the triptych, exploring domestic relationships on metaphysical
and human levels, followed by the autobiographical Intermezzo, which
used the topic of fidelity as material for a light-hearted bourgeois
comedy, and then a return to myth and allegory with Helena. What

links the two bookends of this trilogy is the critical moment when the title roles (the Empress and Helen) take a potentially fatal risk and are thereby forever changed. "Transformation is the life of life itself," Hofmannsthal observed, "the real mystery of nature as creative force. Whoever wants to live must surpass himself, must transform himself: he has to forget. And yet all human merit is linked with permanence, unforgetfulness, constancy." This paradox is explored with great poignancy in what Hofmannsthal considered his finest libretto, his last completed opera text for Strauss.

Die ägyptische Helena premiered in Dresden in June 1928 under Fritz Busch, but not with Jeritza in the title role, even though it was created with her in mind. Instead, Helen was introduced by Elisabeth Rethberg, a "worse than mediocre actress," according to Hofmannsthal. Jeritza followed, five days later, for the Vienna premiere under Strauss, and months later she repeated the role for the Metropolitan Opera in New York. Strauss was, without a doubt, still one of the most famous living composers, with opera directors all over the world scheduling performances of his new opera – some twenty during the first year. But productions of *Helena* dropped off dramatically thereafter, and the work essentially dropped from sight. Strauss and Hofmannsthal were convinced that this opera – with its significant staging difficulties, complex plot, and casting problems – would ultimately come around as had *Ariadne* and *Die Frau ohne Schatten*. But neither would see such a day with *Helena*, despite some changes made in 1933 by Clemens Krauss, with the authorization and cooperation of the composer.

At the time of the *Helena* premiere, a year before the Wall Street Crash of 1929, reactionary forces were gaining strength in Europe. In Italy Mussolini had already been in power for nearly six years, and in Germany Paul von Hindenburg (the nationalistic former field marshal), was elected president in 1925 – a clear signal that Germany was looking backward to past glories in the midst of present instability. That same year the Nazi party was re-established with the goal of broadening its base well beyond Munich. The first

Nuremberg rally was held in 1927, the year in which Hitler completed *Mein Kampf*, and in 1928 the National Socialists gained a small but important foothold in the Reichstag, which – with a polarized right and left wing – had been unable to form a majority coalition for years. In Austria the political center was likewise dangerously eroding in the late 1920s, and the struggle between the right-wing Christian Socialists and the left-wing Social Democrats often broke out into physical violence.

For so many artists and intellectuals of Strauss's generation, such political turbulence was seen as a vindication of their skepticism about a post-war democratic republic. Their skepticism was rooted in the nineteenth-century German-Romantic notion that art, or *Kultur*, was essentially above politics. This view of art and the artist as being nonpolitical was anchored in a uniquely German concept of *Innerlichkeit* (with its emphasis on *Bildung*, on the inner development of the individual) that was simultaneously pro-nation and anti-state. In a 1922 lecture for the Institute of Politics the pro-democracy philosopher-theologian Ernst Troeltsch explained these roots and how they differed from Western European thought:

> The basis of Western political thinking . . . was the view of all men
> forming a single society . . . governed by a common law, *jus naturale*;
> but this had never in modern times been congenial to the German
> mind. In England and America, the idea of Natural Law had inspired
> the demand for personal liberty and for the right of the people to
> control the leaders they had themselves chosen; in France, it had
> become a theory of direct self-government, equality, and full
> participation in the control of the State. Such ideas had never taken
> root in Germany, largely because of the failure of the Enlightenment,
> and the mainstream of German philosophical thought had
> subsequently rejected "the universal egalitarian ethic."[12]

Thus, for Troeltsch the French Enlightenment – which sought to connect philosophy and politics, to merge the needs of the individual with those of the state – had simply passed over Germany, where politics continued to be eyed with skepticism. Art, music, literature existed in a sacred space removed from the everyday, political world. The German *nation*, as cultural phenomenon, could give birth to an individual, but the German *state*, the product of consensus and compromise, could only rob artists of their individuality. This dialectical relationship of "Individual vs. Nation" (but not State) was a highly organic relationship resolved, or synthesized, through *Bildung*: the journey from the part to the whole. Thomas Mann articulated this view in his *Reflections of a Non-Political Man* (1918), but where Mann ultimately reversed his opinion in 1922, embracing democracy and the Weimar Republic, Strauss held on to his Nietzschean beliefs that Christianity and democracy were ideas at odds with individuality, that they reduced the individual to a herd mentality.

National Socialism well illustrated the inherent dangers in this apolitical attitude, with its reactionary or anarchistic tendencies, but, as we shall see in the next chapter, it would be all too easy to distort any link between Strauss and the Nazis by way of Nietzsche or any political ideology. So much of this amateur philosophizing was carried on in a political vacuum, for Strauss himself was no less skeptical of the National Socialists, who in the late twenties he viewed as marginal, uncultured, and illiterate. His later official twenty-month relationship with the Nazi government, from 1934 to 1935, was the result not of ideological sympathy but of simple pragmatism, self-interest, and expediency. Strauss may have distrusted democracy, but he equally distrusted the emerging National Socialist movement, referring, in 1930, to Hitler as a "criminal" and an "ignoramus."[13] Indeed, his distaste for the Nazis would serve as a major source of friction between Strauss and his son, Franz, who early on actually viewed the rise of Hitler with a sense of optimism.

On one level, Strauss could no doubt feel justified in his distrust of contemporary German politics, given the economic turmoil and intense political polarization of the time. His primary focus was not on current events, but on the possibility of another operatic collaboration with Hofmannsthal, a collaboration that would look back to the world of *Rosenkavalier*. In 1922, the year that Hofmannsthal had first devised the plan for a mythological operetta, Strauss had also expressed a desire to write a "second *Rosenkavalier*, but without the mistakes and *longeurs*! You'll just have *to write that for me some day*: I haven't spoken my last word yet in that genre."[14] *Die ägyptische Helena* had failed to satisfy Strauss's desire for an operatic comedy; now he hoped to get his chance.

Arabella, the marvelous fruit of this late labor of the two great artists, would come far closer to the ideal of operetta than *Helena* and, unlike its predecessor, remains one of the most successful late-Hofmannsthal operas. The work revisits Vienna, not however the city of Maria Theresa, but the Vienna of the 1860s, during the rise of liberalism, the so-called *Ringstrasse*-era, a time when Vienna experienced a spectacular building boom and the arts reached an apex of creative florescence. In constructing his libretto, Hofmannsthal returned to two of his earlier works: an unfinished play called *Der Fiaker als Graf* (The Cabby as Count) and a short story entitled "Lucidor." The play provided the setting and atmosphere (especially the *Fiakerball*), but the essence of the story came from "Lucidor," which, however, focused more on Arabella's sister, Zdenka, than on Arabella herself. Strauss did not mind the fact that there were two sopranos; he had delighted in composing music for such paired voices as Ariadne–Zerbinetta, Empress–Dyer's Wife, and Helena–Aithra, but in all of these cases the title role was clearly articulated. Strauss, therefore, sent back Hofmannsthal's first draft asking that Arabella be given a soliloquy to close Act I, and Hofmannsthal's solution delighted the composer. So pleased was Strauss that he immediately sent a telegram of congratulations on 15 July 1929. This euphoria was sadly interrupted by tragedy. Two days earlier, Hofmannsthal's son had shot himself, and on the 15th, Strauss's librettist suffered a massive stroke while preparing for the funeral. His collaborator and artistic inspiration of two decades never opened the telegram.

Strauss, profoundly shaken, was too distraught to attend the funeral (Franz and Alice represented him at the ceremony), but he sent a moving condolence letter to Hofmannsthal's widow:

This genius, this great poet, this sensitive collaborator, this unique talent! No musician ever found such a helper and supporter. No one will ever replace him for me or the world of music!

For the first time in his life, the 65-year-old Strauss – who had such resilience through so many setbacks – seemed unable to emerge from depression. The normally stoic, reserved composer suddenly burst into unrestrained tears while reading aloud from Hofmannsthal's text to Elisabeth Schumann and her husband Carl Alwin, who were paying a condolence visit to Garmisch the day after the poet's death. Over the ensuing months Strauss came to feel increasingly isolated, even disoriented, convinced that his career as an opera composer had come to an end.

The decade had begun with the buoyant Strauss rising from the ashes of Berlin after the war, appointed as a celebrity co-director in Vienna. That directorship, which rested on the shaky foundation of financial instability and personal malice, culminated in Strauss's bitter resignation, yet the Phoenix-like composer rose again, seeing an opportunity to renew his artistic relationship with Hofmannsthal. Having finished Die ägyptische Helena, Strauss was now convinced he could recapture the make-believe world of Der Rosenkavalier. But that all changed in 1929, a year that saw not only the death of his prized librettist but the advent of world-wide economic depression. In Germany, economic collapse brought about dramatic gains for the right, particularly the National Socialists. After their ultimate success in 1933, an over-confident Strauss would learn soon enough that playing the role of non-political artist while simultaneously cultivating ties with the new regime would be a difficult, not to say treacherous task.

5 After Hofmannsthal: personal and political crises

The 1930s, Strauss's most prolific decade as an opera composer, was a period fraught with crisis. Indeed, the steadiness of his output (five operas in ten years) contrasts sharply with the instability of his personal and professional life during this tumultuous decade. In the wake of Hofmannsthal's sudden death in June 1929, an anguished Strauss was convinced he would never write another stage work. For him, no living librettist could match Hofmannsthal's literary depth, his sense of theater, his instinct for musical possibilities. Strauss was cognizant of *Arabella*'s shortcomings, he knew that the text for Acts II and III – which lacked the dramatic focus of Act I – were in need of revision by another hand, but he simply could not bring himself to change what Hofmannsthal had written. Dramaturgical flaws notwithstanding, *Arabella* would be the composer's final tribute to his departed collaborator.

Throughout his life Strauss instinctively turned to work, diligence, and discipline to overcome adversity, and indeed within days of Hofmannsthal's funeral, which he could not bear to attend, Strauss began sketching Act I. But felicitous musical ideas did not come easily; the short score to the first act was not complete until the following summer, with many starts and stops along the way. During moments of creative block, such as he was experiencing with *Arabella*, Strauss found it helpful to undertake less ambitious projects and was thus delighted when the conductor Clemens Krauss asked him to consider reworking Mozart's *Idomeneo* for a new production in Vienna. Krauss, who had succeeded Schalk at the State Opera in 1929, was an enthusiastic supporter of Strauss's music, and the two men would soon form an increasingly strong friendship that would last the rest of the composer's life.

Idomeneo was not Strauss's first reworking of an eighteenth-century opera, for during his Weimar period, the 26-year-old composer had arranged Gluck's *Iphigenie en Tauride* for the German stage, translating the text himself, telescoping four acts into three, and recasting many of the recitatives. *Idomeneo*, moreover, occupied a special place in the heart of a composer who prized Mozart above all others. The work had premiered in Munich in 1781 at the Residenztheater, the very theater where Strauss and his Intendant Ernst von Possart had begun their own Mozart revival in 1896. Lothar Wallerstein, Intendant at the Vienna State Opera, translated the text of Mozart's *opera seria*, and Strauss reworked most of the *secco* recitatives as *accompagnato*, thus creating a more continuous symphonic effect. The composer took particular delight in weaving important referential, quasi-leitmotivic material into these recitatives as well. The arias were mostly untouched, although some were repositioned or cut entirely, and Electra was excised from the plot, perhaps because that character had been so thoroughly explored in his opera of 1908. Nonetheless, Strauss was remarkably true to Mozart's style, with one significant exception: an inserted, newly composed *interludio* near the end of Act II, where a sea monster is presented. Purists, such as Alfred Einstein, predictably denounced the production as a sacrilege, but it was well received by the audience and sympathetic critics and has continued to be revived.

Another small project, originally dating back to 1931, remains the center of a confused controversy, namely Strauss's *Olympic Hymn* for the 1936 games in Berlin.[1] The decision for Germany to host the Olympic games predated Hitler by a few years and was spearheaded by Theodor Lewald, president of the German Olympic Committee. World War I precluded a German Olympiad in 1916, and in 1930

Lewald petitioned for Berlin as the site for the 1936 games. The IOC gave the green light in 1931, and Lewald informally approached Strauss with the request for a choral work to open the games. Strauss expressed willingness, and he received a formal invitation in 1934. A year before, with the arrival of the National Socialists – who took an early isolationist stance – an international event was not altogether certain, and negotiations between Hitler and Lewald, whose father was a Jew, were extremely awkward, not to say politically charged. The search for a hymn text took the form of a national contest, with Strauss choosing from the three finalists, the winner being Robert Lubahn, a civil servant and sometime poet. Strauss put the commissioned work together quite quickly in 1934, and a hazy but heated political context unfortunately has elevated this unremarkable work, which extolls international cooperation, to a level it hardly deserves.

The composer had far more important projects on his mind; the most important one of the early 1930s was finishing *Arabella*. For better or worse, he was determined to set the text to Acts II and III just as Hofmannsthal had left it, the inherent dramaturgical weaknesses notwithstanding. Yet despite those problems, especially the abrupt ending of Act II, Strauss created an opera of compelling lyricism and poignancy. In his libretto, Hofmannsthal was able to avoid most of the heavy psychological elements that had pervaded *Die Frau ohne Schatten* and *Die ägyptische Helena*, which – we recall from the previous chapter – had been originally intended as a mythological operetta. *Arabella*, though not an operetta, certainly has the atmosphere of the lighter genre: a mysterious Croatian count, an Act II ballroom scene, the coloratura Fiakermilli, and sexual intrigue.

Strauss succeeds almost entirely in avoiding the dreaded "Wagnerian musical armor," with a light conversational style reminiscent of *Intermezzo*, interspersed with soaring lyrical moments often infused with the flavor of Croatian folk music. The famous Act I duet between Arabella and her sister, Zdenka, quotes literally from a South Croatian folk song, as does the Act II duet between Arabella and her future husband Mandryka. But the greatest moment of all is the final scene of the work, which opens with a downward sweep in the orchestra in a musical gesture recalling Strauss's lied "Allerseelen." Arabella, who is falsely suspected by Mandryka of infidelity and is now vindicated, descends the staircase to offer her betrothed a glass of pure water. It is a gesture supposedly based on folk custom, yet despite this act of pre-marital submission, Arabella is a character who fully controls her fate throughout the opera. She is "an entirely modern character," according to Hofmannsthal, who in the final line of the piece tells Mandryka that she can only be herself: "Take me as I am."

The score was completed in October 1932, one month before the National Socialists suffered a significant but temporary political defeat. In July they had shocked the world with their 13.5 million votes and 230 seats in the Reichstag, creating an anti-parliamentary majority that posed a threat to minority Chancellor Franz von Papen, conservative head of the Centrist Party. But in November 1932, the Nazis lost 2 million votes and 34 seats, and many believed that with their failure to win an outright majority their high-water mark had been reached. Strauss, who rarely mentioned political events in his calendar, wrote with naive optimism three days after the election, "Hitler seems finished."

With increasing street violence and a crumbling cabinet, von Papen was far more concerned about a possible Communist takeover than one by the Nazis, and he struck a deal that would make Hitler Chancellor, with von Papen keeping things in check as Vice Chancellor. But as von Papen would soon learn, Hitler was not being used: it was quite the other way around. With the burning of the Reichstag in February 1933, the passage of the "enabling laws," and the death of President Hindenburg, the Weimar Republic was finished; the National Socialists soon wielded absolute power.

Hitler had skillfully exploited fear over hope, which was admittedly in short supply during the 1920s; with compelling intuition, he recognized how group prejudice could outweigh class identity. Social divisions were, therefore, glossed over through the indoctrination of age-old ethnic prejudices, by exploiting time-honored notions of the "other," the natural-born enemies of a nostalgic, mythical *Volk*. Such opponents included leftists, pacifists, intellectuals, and artists, but the principal group allegedly responsible for Germany's misery – for the "stab in the back" at Versailles – were the Jews. Depending on their audience, Nazi politicians could characterize Jews as greedy capitalists (entrepeneurs importing foreign culture for monetary gain) on the one hand or as dangerous anti-capitalist leftists (Bolshevist followers of the Jewish Karl Marx) on the other.

Like many other Germans of his generation, Franz Strauss, the composer's son, greeted the new regime with enthusiasm, despite the fact that he had a Jewish wife. Indeed, his optimism concerning the new government was the source of many heated arguments between father and son. In the first year of the National Socialists, before the Nuremberg laws and the realities of *Reichskristallnacht*, it was difficult if not impossible to understand or predict the ultimate extent of Nazi anti-Semitism, or even to know whether the National Socialists would stay in power. What was easy to understand was that large numbers of Jews were dismissed from their positions within the first months of the new regime, and these dismissals were often swift and humiliating. Bruno Walter, for example, arrived for a scheduled rehearsal with his Leipzig Gewandhaus Orchestra in March 1933 only to find that he was literally locked out of the hall. Organized groups stormed concert halls and opera houses, and smoke bombs would interrupt performances.

Fritz Busch, music director of the Dresden Opera, experienced one such evening as he was about to conduct *Rigoletto* in March 1933. Busch, who was not Jewish, had been an early and outspoken critic of the new regime, and local SA officers eagerly sought revenge. They bought up blocks of tickets for *Rigoletto* and staged a demonstration that did not end until Busch was replaced in the opera pit by Kurt Striegler, a second-rate crony who had been waiting in the wings all evening. Strauss had been greatly impressed with Busch's premiere of *Die ägyptische Helena* in Dresden, so much so that he dedicated *Arabella* to him and his Dresden Intendant Alfred Reucker. It was also a clear message that the Busch–Reucker team should also produce his new opera, which was slated for a July 1933 premiere.

With Busch's dismissal from Dresden, Strauss tried to have the premiere moved to a venue where Busch could conduct, but it was impossible for the composer to get out of a contract that he had already signed, and the first performance took place under Clemens Krauss. It was a great success, to Strauss's surprise, but one covered by the cloud of National Socialism (and its most immediate effects) as well as the absence of *Arabella*'s librettist, Hofmannsthal. Göring tried to keep Busch in Germany by holding out the possibility of a Berlin appointment, but when that did not come through, he left Germany for good. Strauss was greatly pained that *Arabella*'s dedicatee was unable to conduct its premiere, and it was not until after the war that Busch realized how hard Strauss had tried to get out of his contract. The composer and his attorney son, Franz, had even gone to Berlin to negotiate with the government about breaking the contract, but to no avail. "I am entirely hopeless with this cursed contract," he wrote in his calendar after the trip to the German capital. His anguish about the *Arabella* affair did not abate until he was able to resume ties with Busch right after the war.

On the other hand, the composer's despair at losing his favorite librettist had eased considerably by 1931, when by chance he made the acquaintance of the Austrian writer Stefan Zweig. Strauss recalled:

> When I had just about given up hope of ever finding a librettist again, I was visited by Anton Kippenberg of Insel-Verlag, who was on his way to Stefan Zweig in Salzburg . . . Casually I said to Kippenberg: Why don't you ask Zweig (whom I did not know in person) whether he has an opera subject for me. That was in the winter of 1931–1932. Presently I got a letter from Zweig, saying he did in fact have some thoughts but until now had not been bold enough to present them to me.[2]

For a couple of years Strauss had looked in vain for a suitable librettist. Hans Bethge, translator of the Chinese poems (*Die chinesische Flöte*) for Mahler's *Das Lied von der Erde* and poet for Strauss's Op. 77 *Gesänge des*

Orients, sent Strauss an opera scenario entitled *The Laughter of the Empress*, but it failed to make an impression. In late 1929, Alma Mahler paid a visit with her second husband, Franz Werfel, in the hope that Strauss might be able to form a collaboration, but to no avail. Of course, the composer's mailbox was also regularly filled with unsolicited manuscripts from writers hoping to make a connection with fame. In the end, Strauss was left with nothing until late October when he received a letter from Zweig, who had been prodded by Kippenberg.

Zweig had two proposals: a dance-pantomime "in the grand style" and a "cheerful, lively *Spieloper*." Author and composer met for the first time on 20 November at the Hotel Vier Jahreszeiten in Munich and discussed the proposals at length. Strauss opted for the opera project, ultimately known as *Die schweigsame Frau*, which was to be the only comic opera by Strass in an authentic *buffa* tradition. If the period of work on *Arabella* marked some of Strauss's darkest moments, this new project, which brought him into a collaboration with another gifted Austrian writer, was one of the brightest. Not since *Der Rosenkavalier* had Strauss shown such unbridled enthusiasm for a libretto, which he declared to be "a born comic opera . . . more suitable for music than even *Figaro* and the *Barber of Seville*." Strauss had yet to find his true comic opera after *Rosenkavalier*, for the light-hearted projects by Hofmannsthal had all become more complex and psychological by the end of each collaboration – even, to a certain extent, *Arabella*. Zweig, for once, offered Strauss pure fun.

Based on Ben Jonson's *The Silent Woman* (1609), the text shares an affinity not so much with Mozart or Rossini as with Donizetti, especially his *Don Pasquale* of 1843. Both Pasquale and Morosus, the leading male role in *Die schweigsame Frau*, are crotchety old bachelors upon whom friends and relatives play good-natured tricks. There are numerous and amusing allusions to Italian operas, in both text and music, throughout an opera that represents some of Strauss's lightest music for the stage. Indeed, the steady *parlante* style, with only rare moments of lyricism, has made this opera – especially for non-

German-speaking audiences – somewhat tedious. Strauss was, none-theless, delighted with the result and always considered it one of his best stage comedies.

With the three-act libretto completed by late January 1933, Strauss was ready to begin composing – and quickly at that: the entire score was finished by 1934. Strauss could not believe his good fortune; he had found his second "Da Ponte and Scribe rolled into one," a writer of international stature, who like Hofmannsthal also had a profound knowledge of music. Strauss saw a long bright future with this new collaborator. On 29 January 1933, with full libretto in hand, he was ready to draw up a formal agreement with Zweig: 25 percent of the roy-alties from stage productions, 20 percent from the book, as well as the autograph copy of the particell. Strauss added:

> I believe it will be necessary for you, as a librettist, to join the
> Association of German Composers in Berlin to insure that you'll
> receive your share from concert performances of fragments with
> lyrics of our opera, also from records and movies.[3]

Two days later Hitler became Chancellor, and neither Strauss nor Zweig, a Jew, had any idea what this event would mean to their artistic relationship.

Strauss's relationship with the National Socialist government during the 1930s was complex, intricate and resists easy answers. Over the decades following the Second World War the picture of Strauss during the Third Reich has remained obscured either by uncritical rationalizing and omission by Straussian sympathizers or by polemical, selective simplistic accusations by those unsympathetic to the composer. One thing is clear: Strauss showed little courageous opposition during this grim twelve-year period. Especially in the first three years of the regime we can trace a pattern of cooperation and accommodation, a pattern drawn in part from his earlier dealings with political authorities: dukes, Kaisers, presidents, and chancel-lors. But neither was he a Nazi sympathizer, nor did he share their anti-Semitic beliefs. Strauss was a composer who, up until 1933, had always been able to put his life above politics. This tactic of positioning oneself outside the political realm, while simultaneously exploiting political structures for artistic gain, would produce serious consequences with the arrival of the new government in 1933.

The Toscanini episode in Bayreuth served as an unfortunate case in point. Following the deaths of Cosima and Siegfried Wagner in 1930, Strauss – who had been estranged from the Wagner family since the turn of the century – saw the opportunity to repair decades of bad relations and began to cultivate friendly relations with Winifred Wagner, who became head of the Bayreuth Festival. After Toscanini canceled his *Parsifal* contract as an act of political protest, Strauss was asked by Winifred to step in as his replacement. The composer no doubt saw the chance for another gesture of goodwill toward Wahnfried, when the 1933 festival marked the fiftieth anniversary of the composer's death.

Strauss may have donated his fee to a festival badly in need of money, but he plainly ignored the fact that it played right into the hands of a National Socialist regime eagerly seeking international legitimacy during its first year in power. Was it irony or denial that led him to observe: "It is nice, for once, to live entirely in art and to hear nothing about politics" on the day of his arrival at the festival, a festival that was swirling in politics? The same can be said of Strauss's replacing Bruno Walter, who was essentially forbidden to conduct the Berlin Philharmonic in March 1933. After much pleading from Luise Wolff, concert agent for the orchestra, Strauss first refused but finally agreed to stand in, donating his fee to the cash-needy orchestra that he had helped build. But for all that he paid a much higher price in damage to his reputation, especially after the war.

Strauss conducted his first *Parsifal* on 22 July, and during the second intermission Winifred Wagner introduced the composer to Hitler. Strauss used the opportunity to discuss copyright reform, permission to travel to Austria, theatrical subventions from film and radio receipts, and the problem of Jews being dismissed from their positions. In particular, he spoke out on behalf of his good friend Leo

Blech, the prominent conductor and the man who introduced Strauss to Emanuel von Grab, the future father-in-law of Franz Strauss. The Nazis had closed the Austrian border to Germans, and Strauss was anxious that he might not be able to conduct at the Salzburg Festival that summer as well as miss the Vienna premiere of his *Arabella* in the fall.

Strauss was among many artists, of various political beliefs, who held out early hope that the cultural scene might actually improve with the downfall of the Weimar Republic, whose cultural administration had been in a state of confusion in the late 1920s and early 1930s. The composer claimed to have been in "high spirits" that Hitler agreed with his "ideal goals"; the Weimar government had ignored his request concerning copyright extension and subventions for German theaters.

Any optimism concerning the Jewish question was surely wishful thinking on the part of Strauss. He was, however, finally permitted to go to Salzburg that summer where he conducted *Fidelio* and a revised *Die ägyptische Helena*, and he also attended Vienna's first *Arabella* in October joined by Hofmannsthal's widow, Engelbert Dollfuss, Kurt Schuschnigg, Franz Lehár, and – curiously – Arturo Toscanini. Earlier that month Strauss traveled to Berlin to discuss changes in the copyright law with Minister of Propaganda Joseph Goebbels, who had tremendous control over the cultural scene in the Third Reich. For years Strauss had tried to extend copyright protection for composers from thirty to fifty years after their death. During the Weimar years Strauss sought to have the law changed but was largely ignored; Goebbels, eager to form an alliance with Germany's most famous composer, lent a sympathetic ear.

Indeed, the following month Goebbels sent Strauss a telegram asking him to become president of the recently formed Reichsmusikkammer. The composer accepted, joined by Wilhelm Furtwängler as deputy, and a council was formed consisting of Furtwängler, Gustav Havemann, Fritz Stein, Paul Graener, Heinz Ihlert, and Gerd Kernbach. Thus, at the top of the hierarchy were non-party, high-profile music professionals, such as Strauss and Furtwängler, along with party ideologues filling in at middle and lower levels. Strauss, who as co-director in Vienna had shown little or no interest in day-to-day operations, saw himself as a figure-head, but one with enough influence to be able to implement long-standing cultural goals, goals that never saw fruition in the 1920s. Beyond the issue of composers' rights, he wanted to upgrade musical training not only at conservatories but at the primary and secondary school levels as well, where theory and harmony would be offered at a young age. He also wanted to eliminate patriotic and marching songs in the schools and youth organizations, which he found to be a public nuisance with the potential to ruin adolescent voices. Strauss also saw the opportunity to create tighter artistic control over German opera houses, suggesting that the German repertoire be increased, and he wanted to improve the quality of radio music programming as well.

It was an ambitous, unrealistic list of objectives, and in the end all that he was able to achieve during his short presidential tenure was the copyright extension. Strauss, who in the past had successfully manipulated politicians to achieve his goals, was in the end the one who was manipulated. Goebbels's flattery and the offer of artistic control at the national level were hard for the composer to resist, but Strauss, who paradoxically enjoyed the role of a composer above politics, would soon realize the difficulty of maintaining an apolitical stance with this new regime.

The presidential appointment was in fact doomed from the start: Strauss insisted on a hands-off presidency, coming to Berlin only when necessary, and he had no interest in ideological issues of race or censorship. He also found himself in the position of undoing embarrassing political decisions made by second-rank ideologues of the Music Chamber. Goebbels and other high officials of the Reich Culture Chamber were soon disappointed with what they viewed as a narrow, self-serving composer. Just as in Vienna during the early 1920s, Strauss's absence from day-to-day administration – preferring Garmisch to Berlin – gave the opportunity for subordinates to undermine his image. He was accused of being a "non-player" who surrounded himself with Jews and half-Jews: his publisher, his librettists, even his daughter-in-law and grandchildren.

As president of the Music Chamber Strauss also believed that he could insure the performances of his Hofmannsthal operas – despite the librettist's Jewish ancestry – and that the premiere of his *Die schweigsame Frau* would go forward notwithstanding its Jewish librettist. And he was right. None of the operas from *Elektra* through *Arabella* suffered, and *Die schweigsame Frau* cleared Nazi censors, with a premiere scheduled for Dresden in June 1935. Hitler and Goebbels even promised to attend. But the more Strauss tried to ignore political events around him, the more politics invaded his world, a world he believed to be removed from the rules of the regime. As he neared the completion of *Die schweigsame Frau* and began thinking about future projects, Strauss refused to accept the fact that a Jew could no longer be his collaborator. The composer's negative reaction to Nazi anti-Semitism is revealing in this instance, for he dwelt not so much on its global evil but on how it affected his career. In an impassioned letter to Zweig (17 June 1935), Strauss candidly expressed his opinions of Nazi ideology:

> Do you believe that I am ever, in any of my actions, guided by the thought that I am "German" ... Do you believe that Mozart composed as an Aryan? I know only two types of people: those with and without talent. The people [das Volk] exist for me only at the moment they become audience. Whether they are Chinese, Bavarians, New Zealanders, or Berliners leaves me cold. What matters is that they pay full price of admission.[4]

Strauss also claimed to be "miming" this "troublesome honorary office," which he would have accepted under previous governments, but "neither Kaiser Wilhelm nor Herr [Walter] Rathenau offered it to me."

Zweig never got this letter, which was intercepted by the Gestapo, who had been spying on Strauss, and opening his mail, for some time.

A copy of the letter was sent directly to Hitler two weeks later, and both the Führer and Goebbels were livid. But at the same time Goebbels surely experienced an inner delight, for he had wanted to get rid of Strauss for months, and now he had an excuse. Strauss was called to Berchtesgaden and told to resign immediately from the office he had held for twenty months. *Die schweigsame Frau*, which premiered a week after the Gestapo intercepted the letter, was canceled after only four performances.

The year 1935 was an important turning point in the life of Strauss, a man who had outlived the reigns of a king, three Kaisers, and several governments of the Weimar Republic, a composer whose long-standing fame had allowed him to operate at times outside the political structure. That all changed with the harsh realities of July 1935, when he suddenly realized his impotence with respect to the present government, one unlike any other he had known. Like so many during the first years of the regime, Strauss failed to comprehend fully the significance of Nazi racial policies. Before 1935 he had seen anti-Semitism handed out in an arbitrary, often capricious way, and he never dreamt that his family would ever be affected. Indeed, in May he had sent his daughter-in-law an unsealed art postcard from Kassel (Rembrandt's "Jacob Blesses his Grandson") with the sarcastic annotation: "Not yet forbidden by Rosenberg." Alfred Rosenberg had been the party's top cultural ideologue since 1929. Strauss's naive optimism changed with the passing of the Nuremberg laws in 1935, which formally stripped Jews of their rights as citizens. Marriage between Aryans and Jews – such as between Franz and Alice Strauss – was forbidden, and the composer's daughter-in-law and two grandsons were no longer full citizens of the Reich.

Goebbels once remarked to Strauss that "the world is not as you see it from your Garmisch study," and that world finally caved in on Strauss, whose major goal in life had been creating financial security for his family. How would mere subjects of the Reich be able to get a proper education or hold decent jobs? From 1935 onward, Strauss never achieved any lasting peace of mind in matters concerning his family. Alice was to be spat upon in public, the grandchildren were to have stones thrown at them, but things would get even worse for them after the *Reichskristallnacht* of November 1938. Shortly after being fired from his post in 1935, Strauss wrote an obeisant letter to Hitler requesting an immediate audience to explain the letter to Zweig, but the Führer, further determined to humiliate the composer, never answered him, and the silence must have been deafening. Though the Nazis could easily have made a blanket decision to protect Strauss's family and home, they did not, forcing the composer to seek such protection on a case-by-case basis for the duration of the Reich. "The strategy was to use and abuse the composer at one and the same time," Michael Kater observes, "to make him pay for the sins of the past and nip further rebellion in the bud."[5]

To insure his protection, Strauss no longer had allies at the top of the Nazi hierarchy; he could only find help at the next level. Baldur von Schirach, the head of the Hitler Youth and later Gauleiter of Vienna, came from a musical family with personal musical knowledge that was extensive; he had admired Strauss's music all his life. Hans Frank, the infamous Nazi Governor-General of Poland, was likewise a life-long admirer, and Strauss's friend, Heinz Tietjen, Intendant in Berlin, had close ties to Göring. Strauss would come to depend on these figures in numerous ways to protect his family from various types of harm.

Though the commission of the *Olympic Hymn* had nothing to do with the Nazi government, Strauss believed that, by conducting it himself in the Berlin stadium, he might repair relations with the upper government hierarchy, but that gesture failed to do so. He later composed the *Japanese Festival Music* (1940) hoping that the Japanese might intercede on his behalf in Berlin, but there is no evidence that such leverage was ever used. At age seventy-one, Strauss had reached a moment of grave personal and artistic crisis: beset by worries about his family and about ever finding another librettist. Every writer suggested by Zweig (Rudolf Binding, Robert Faesi, and Alexander Lernet-Holenia) brought only derisive replies from Strauss. The suggestion (in April 1935) of Joseph Gregor, a distinguished Austrian theater historian who wrote plays on the side, was met with equal irritation from Strauss. But after a six-week period of special pleading by Zweig – and the promise that he would look over everything that Gregor wrote – Strauss, resigned to the fact that Zweig was out of the picture, agreed to meet him.

Indeed, they met in Berchtesgaden on 7 July, the day after Strauss was told of his dismissal. Gregor reported that he showed the composer six proposals:

> I still remember, with great precision, that he did not read any of the pages more than approximately two minutes, and he did not read any a second time. Rather he had already put three drafts aside, drafts that he indicated to me had dramatic themes that would interest him. Thus, in a short quarter of an hour, the working program for the next four years was established.[6]

What these six proposals actually were remains unclear, but if we follow the logic of Gregor's account, the four-year "working program" probably included Der Friedenstag, Daphne, and Die Liebe der Danae.

Strauss was unimpressed with Gregor's work; he had already seen a libretto proposal (Semiramis) before their meeting, and for summer 1935 he postponed any operatic plans, opting for a work for men's chorus, the Drei Männerchöre (1935) based on poems by Friedrich Rückert. Pauline described Strauss as being in the "deepest depression," and his turn to Rückert might be seen as a way of assuaging his bleak state of mind, a means of turning his attention away from the turmoil that surrounded him. He had set a Rückert poem for a cappella double chorus earlier in the year (Die Göttin im Putzzimmer) and, of course, his more ambitious Op. 62 Deutsche Motette (1913) for four soloists and sixteen-part chorus is a setting of Rückert's "Die Schöpfung ist zur Ruh gegangen."

Though the last of the Drei Männerchöre ("Happiness in May") seems escapist given its context, the first two weeks reflect compellingly

Strauss's grim state of mind. The first Rückert poem, "Before the Doors," tells of an individual knocking at the houses of prosperity, love, honor, and contentment, and each approach is thwarted. But then he recalls:

> Yet I now know a little quiet house,
> Where I may finally knock.
> Where, indeed, many guests stay:
> The grave offers rest for many.

Of the three choruses, this one is the most nihilistic, where only the grave can offer a final refuge for a world-weary artist traveling from place to place. The second – and more serene – chorus, "Dream Light," is about a visionary light that fleetingly visits the narrator during his sleep: "O star come often during my rest. For you I gladly close my eyes." But as in the first poem, the poet seeks solace by rejecting the outer world, where death is equated with ultimate rest.

Far more revealing, however, are two other Rückert choruses that never got beyond early musical sketches. In these texts we clearly recognize both Strauss's disgust with the state of German politics as well as his fear of impending war. It is difficult not to think about the Nazis in Rückert's "Inner Peace," a poem that laments a world taken over by a dark force (the emphasis is by Strauss):

> How the world might be redeemed
> From this force that so constricts
> Her heart's blood, I do not know,
> But that this must be achieved
> Her anxious gestures now betray it
> Even if *no tongue* will say it.
>
> Down with deception, down with lies,
> Away with all the stratagems
> So that what's known as politics
> And feeds pathetically on them
> Misleads none other than itself
> Not *its opponent, spiritual life.*[7]

"Reconciliation" reflects the composer's anxiety at the thought of war:

> I still see horror's traces
> A hundred-thousand fold –
> The meadow full of corpses,
> The blood in stream and wold,
> And human hands, in infamy,
> Bear spots they'll never wash away.[8]

The Drei Männerchöre are rarely performed – the unfinished sketches for the other two choruses are entirely unknown – but this work stands out as a rare instance of music directly linked to the composer's personal state of mind. Strauss was normally averse to moments of self-reflection or confession in music. In this same pacifist state of mind he composed his next opera, Der Friedenstag (The Day of Peace). Stefan Zweig suggested the original idea, to create an opera about the end of the Thirty Years War and the Peace of Westphalia in 1648, thereby predating the Drei Männerchöre, but it would not be carried out by Zweig. In 1935 Strauss, now in his seventies, finally gave in to Zweig and accepted Joseph Gregor as his collaborator with the understanding that Zweig would help Gregor behind the scenes.

Gregor, the theater historian, was neither a Hofmannsthal nor even a Zweig, but he was all that Strauss had in 1935. This new collaboration was a unique working relationship where the composer assumed almost total artistic control. Strauss, who had learned much about crafting a libretto from Hofmannsthal, could be blunt and occasionally outright insulting in order to achieve the required results. Sometimes he would rewrite passages himself, and he never hesitated to seek the advice of others, principally that of Clemens Krauss, who would later serve as collaborator on his final opera, Capriccio.

Zweig, who promised to assist Gregor "page by page" if necessary, proved true to his word; Friedenstag (originally called 1648) would be Strauss's first one-act opera since Elektra, and it remains unique in the composer's operatic output. Strauss, who throughout his life was inspired chiefly by the female voice, found himself writing music mostly for male singers, and he no doubt drew from his recent experience composing the Rückert men's choruses. The music of *Friedenstag* is dark and brooding, lacking the warmth of his other operas, the only exception being the role of Marie, wife of the steadfast Commandant and the only solo soprano role in the entire work. Ironic musical allusions to the march idiom, in a distinctly Mahlerian guise, suggest the distance between Strauss and his military material. What attracted him to the libretto in the first place was its call for tolerance between opponents, the promise of peace between opposing military forces. After the two enemy commandants embrace, Strauss composed an extended C major choral finale, a conscious allusion to the end of *Fidelio*. The score to this pacifist opera was completed in June 1936, three months after the Germans remilitarized the Rhineland; the premiere took place on 24 July 1938 in Munich, some four months after the annexation of Austria and with "Greater Germany" gearing up for war. After the outbreak of World War II, performances of *Friedenstag* were significantly curtailed, and performances since 1945 have been rare indeed. With its paucity of stage action and extensive choral treatment, the work is perhaps as much a scenic cantata as an opera, and recent productions have been usually performed in concert version.

Immediately following the drafts to the choral finale of *Friedenstag* are sketches to another, though unfinished, work: a three-movement concerto for cello and orchestra. Though Strauss designates it an "authentic cello concerto," the first concerto since the Op. 11 Horn Concerto of 1883, there is a clearly articulated programmatic subtext, a "struggle of the artistic spirit [the cello] against pseudo-heroism, resignation, melancholy [the orchestra]." This artistic spirit – sometimes called *Lebensfreude*, other times *Lebenslust* – is symbolized by the same bright, life-affirming C major key that closed the *Friedenstag* finale. The composer never got beyond preliminary sketches, but the basic thematic material for all three movements is well established.

One may interpret this curious, unfinished work on two strata. On one level, we can make the obvious connection between pseudo-heroism and the Nazi regime, but, on another level, Strauss's "program" betrays a pronounced Nietzschean language, one recalling the later tone poems of the second half of the 1890s, especially *Also sprach Zarathustra* and *Ein Heldenleben*. The former, we recall from chapter two, extols the power of beauty, life, and nature (the key of C), but it is a life constantly undercut by irony, disgust, and self-doubt of humanity (the key of B). In an early sketch for *Heldenleben*, Strauss writes of a hero rising up "in order to confront the inner enemies (doubt, disgust) and the external enemies." In these tone poems, the classic Nietzschean struggle between joy and doubt was conceived on a more abstract level, yet this very struggle takes on a far more concrete, even confessional, tone in the context of the cello concerto, where a resigned, melancholy septuagenarian tried to overcome crises in his personal and artistic life.

The cello concerto was one among various instrumental projects left incomplete. With amazing frankness and detachment, Strauss once admitted to Zweig that composing purely instrumental music was difficult in old age, it required creative freshness and energy. A libretto provided the necessary framework with which he could explore and expand his musical ideas. Other unfinished works included a symphony based on three themes (*Trigon*) from the 1920s and the tone poem *Die Donau*, which got as far as some 400 bars of particell. Indeed, while sketching out his concerto, he was simultaneously collaborating with Gregor on another one-act opera, a work intended to be the second opera of a double bill with *Friedenstag*. For, if *Friedenstag* "expresses the highest idea of man," according to Gregor, the new opera, *Daphne*, should sing "the peace of nature." These two one-act works would be symmetrically linked by choral finales celebrating these very themes.

Daphne, which was Gregor's only original libretto for Strauss, was probably his best. Gregor, who had recently seen a lithograph of Apollo and Daphne by Theodor Chasseriau, was inspired by the depiction of Apollo as an ardent, romantic god in contrast to that of Daphne in all her childlike innocence. The story of Daphne, who according to Ovid's *Metamorphoses* was transformed into a laurel tree, likely reminded Strauss of the Rückert men's chorus ("Inner Peace") that he had left incomplete a year earlier. There the final stanza was about a tree of peace growing heavenward:

> Let this very blade, this palm,
> With its slim and towering stem
> Be the new tree of peace, the balm!
> Watered not with blood, but dew,
> Let it sprout toward heaven's realm
> And its shadow earth o'erwhelm.

Gregor's text is a far cry from Rückert and whatever success he had with the libretto came from much hands-on assistance by Zweig, Strauss, and Clemens Krauss. The text went through three fundamental versions, and the birth process was indeed painful. "The surgeon's saw also hurts," Strauss remarked to Gregor "[especially] when it is used without anesthetic," and the composer's letters to Gregor rarely contained much in the way of anesthesia.

Yet, with the third version a satisfied Strauss was ready to compose, and he progressed steadily until he got to the ending in early spring 1937. Curiously, the only other instance when Strauss had reached an impasse at an operatic close had been *Elektra*, his only other one-act mythological opera. With Hofmannsthal's earlier text, the problem lay in the composer's understanding of the meaning of Elektra's ultimate demise. The problem with the Gregor libretto was on a shallower level, namely its prosaic choral finale. Strauss was interested, above all, in the magic of Daphne's transformation, while his librettist only offered him stiff pageantry.

Without informing Gregor, Struss took the text to his friend Krauss, who put his finger on the problem. The idea of bringing people on stage and singing to a tree was patently absurd, and he suggested that Strauss "close the piece with the visible transformation [of Daphne] and the gradual transition of human language into the

[wordless] voice of nature."⁹ Strauss was elated and wrote Gregor
within days; it was a letter that epitomized their working relationship,
for what the composer offered was less a suggestion than a direct
order: "no other human being but Daphne must appear on stage, no
Peneios, no solo voices – no chorus – in short, no oratorio." He continues:

> In the moonlight, but still fully visible – the miracle of
> transformation occurs: *only with orchestra alone!* At most Daphne
> might speak a few words during the transformation, which turn into
> stuttering and then *wordless* melody!¹⁰

Grudgingly, Gregor made the change, and though it altered his original concept of his double bill where two operas culminated in an
extended chorus (shifting the focus to the very process of transformation), he later admitted that the revised ending "was one of the most
musical inspirations of [Strauss's] genius."

This shift of focus delighted the composer, for the theme of transformation, tranfiguration, and metamorphosis weaved its way
throughout Strauss's music from *Death and Transfiguration* (1890) to
the *Metamorphosen* (1945). We recall that it was a theme close to the
heart of Hofmannsthal as well, and it played a role in one form or
another in nearly all his libretti. Daphne is in many ways the opposite
of the Empress in *Die Frau ohne Schatten* (1919), a character who desires
mortality, who wants to bear children, and through an act of humanity, that of self-sacrifice, she is transformed into a mortal being. The
mortal Daphne, on the other hand, is transformed by Apollo into an
immortal voice of nature. This famous passage, with its soaring melodies, seemingly effortless contrapuntal interplay of returning
motives, skillful harmonic pacing, and mastery of orchestral sound
that is at once rich and refined, is perhaps the most compelling finale
of any late opera by Strauss.

The work was dedicated to Karl Böhm, who had premiered *Die
schweigsame Frau*, with the understanding that he would conduct
the first performance of *Daphne* in Dresden. *Daphne*, which was performed along with *Friedenstag*, would be the last of nine Strauss operas

to be premiered in Dresden, a tradition reaching back to *Feuersnot* in 1901. The evening was a great success, with some forty curtain calls for the new work, though with the inclusion of *Friedenstag* it was a long evening indeed: nearly four hours of music, not including the one intermission. As a result, *Daphne* and the less popular *Friedenstag* soon went their separate ways, and the former continues to be the most successful of the three Gregor operas.

By now, in 1938, Strauss believed he had reached a level of understanding with the government. He attended the Düsseldorf *Reichsmusiktage* in May, where he conducted his *Arabella* and, the following day, his *Festival Prelude*, which preceded a cultural speech by Goebbels. By conducting this work originally written for the opening of the Vienna Konzerthaus in 1913, Strauss thought he finally had reached a reconciliation with the propaganda minister. But if he believed that he had, in any way, assured the protection of his family, he was sadly wrong. One month after the *Daphne* premiere, Strauss – who was in Italy for a concert engagement at La Scala – learned that Alice had been placed under house arrest in Garmisch. She had lost her passport and driver's license, and it was questionable whether or not her sons would be allowed to attend school. Strauss asked Heinz Tietjen, who had close connections with Göring, to use his influence to get him an audience with Hitler to plead on his family's behalf or at least somehow have the orders reversed. On 17 December 1938, he wrote:

> We have had some bitter weeks. Beyond the unstable worries about the future of my two dear grandsons, which I have carried in my heart for years, the fate of my wonderful daughter-in-law . . . has caused me great pain.[11]

A few months later he thanked Tietjen for his help, though nothing had been fully resolved:

> My son is a good fellow, his wife, as I have described to you, a pearl of a woman and the mother of two really wonderful sons! If everything gets rectified according to your wish, you will have freed me and my wife from a great worry.[12]

A seventy-fifth birthday celebration in Vienna gave Strauss the opportunity to have a two-hour discussion at the Hotel Imperial with Goebbels on 11 June 1939, and he reported to Tietjen that they were able to put aside their differences, with the propaganda minister assuring Strauss that he would seek Hitler's protection for his daughter-in-law and grandsons: "With great pain, we await a positive solution!" But the blanket protection from the Führer was never obtained.

All the while Strauss was working on a new opera, something less serious than the recently composed pair of one-act works, and he was reminded, by Willi Schuh (Swiss music critic and future Strauss biographer), of a mythological comedy that Hofmannsthal had sketched shortly before the collaboration on *Die ägyptische Helena*. After the tortuous *Frau ohne Schatten*, Strauss had wanted a lighter, more cheerful work, and Hofmannsthal responded with a scenario called *Danae or the Marriage of Convenience*, a work that conflated two myths: Danae's visitation by Jupiter in the guise of golden rain and the legend of Midas and the golden touch. As much as Strauss admired many details of Hofmannsthal's sketch, there were too many insurmountable dramaturgical problems, and he became increasingly preoccupied with his own *Intermezzo*. *Danae* was soon forgotten. But against the background of the grim personal and political events surrounding Strauss's life, themes of the Thirty Years War and Greek tragedy had taken their toll on the composer, who asked Gregor if he could resurrect the cheerful Hofmannsthal sketch, even though Gregor himself had shown the composer his own *Danae* scenario in 1936. The fragile satire of Hofmannsthal's draft was well beyond Gregor's grasp, whose job was further complicated by the very dramaturgical problems that had vexed Strauss in 1920. Yet after long, diligent work – and much outside assistance – a libretto was finally forged.

Strauss continued to believe in the spiritual power of diligence and work, and he found the composition of *Danae* to be his only solace; the three-act opera was composed with remarkable speed. By early September 1939, while taking a cure in Baden, he began to score Act I, just six days after Germany invaded Poland, setting off the Second World War. With sarcastic resignation, an aged, depressed composer wrote in his calendar: "Declaration of war – it's just as well. In the afternoon [I became] depressed while in the spa garden." As early as his June seventy-fifth birthday celebration in Vienna he had already realized the inevitability of war, which surely explains a rare public outburst of emotion following the end of the birthday performance of the *Symphonia domestica* at the Musikverein:

> At the end he was stormily applauded, but when I met him at the exit from the platform, he suddenly threw the baton away, stumbled into the artists' room, sat down, visibly distressed, and murmured: "Now it's all over," and began to cry bitterly . . . After a short time his son arrived and put his arm around his father, who was growing calmer, and all was well again.[13]

Die Liebe der Danae may have been Strauss's comfort during a time of instability, but with the outbreak of world war, even composing could do little to assuage the composer's fears. Indeed, because of World War II, *Danae* would not be premiered until after Strauss's death. The 1930s had begun with the hope that Strauss had found, in Stefan Zweig, a new librettist; the decade ended with the German invasion of Poland. After the Anschluss of Austria in 1938, Zweig left for London, then sailed to Brazil three years later. In February 1942 he shot himself, leaving a suicide note saluting his friends and colleagues: "May it be granted them yet to see the dawn after the long night! I, all too impatient, go on before." Strauss would ultimately see dawn, but it was a dawn that cast its light on opera houses, concert halls, and museums reduced to rubble. European culture as Strauss had known it had come to an end.

6 "Now the day has made me tired": the War and its aftermath

Strauss's diaries indicate that as early as 1939, with the invasion of Poland, he foresaw the destruction of cultural institutions he had known so intimately all his life. Dispirited and resigned, Strauss began scoring *Die Liebe der Danae* believing that it might well be his final opera. With the outbreak of another world war he was determined that *Danae* should not be premiered until at least two years after an armistice, knowing full well that such terms might mean a posthumous performance. Over time, and after much pressure from his friend Clemens Krauss, the composer finally acceded to a Salzburg premiere during summer 1944. Yet Strauss's original instincts proved correct, for on 1 August, during the summer preparations, Goebbels declared "total war," which meant the immediate closing of all the theaters throughout the Reich. The Gauleiter of Salzburg, with the backing of the Propaganda Minister, made an exception for Strauss, allowing rehearsals to continue so long as there would be no production beyond a final dress rehearsal, which took place (for invited guests) on 16 August 1944. A posthumous premiere, also under Krauss but with a different cast, occurred eight years later in Salzburg.

Political and personal worries had taken their toll during the genesis of this three-act work, which was hardly the "light mythology" that had originally been envisaged. Once a workable libretto was achieved, Strauss composed the music with remarkable speed, and by June 1940 the scoring of this *opera semi-seria* was complete. *Danae*, with its many transformations and demanding vocal parts, is a challenge to stage and to cast, which helps explain the reason it is rarely performed. The title role is written for Krauss's wife, Viorica Ursuleac, a role with ample instances of the quiet, sustained high-ranged singing for which she was famous. Equally difficult is the role of Jupiter, a *tour de force* in the Straussian baritone repertoire, for not only is the range significantly high (sections were transposed even for the premiere) but it demands great vocal agility, especially in the final "Maia Erzählung," one of the finest baritone monologues that Strauss ever composed. Despite the various contributors to the libretto beyond Gregor (Krauss, Zweig, Lothar Wallerstein), one detects the spirit of Hofmannsthal in its broad themes that recall *Die ägyptische Helena* with its focus on marriage, fidelity, and memory. In the end Danae chooses love over money and power; Jupiter, who had tried to lure her away, renounces all earthly things and, after blessing the union of Danae and Midas, he returns to Olympus. The eighty-year-old Strauss strongly identified with the resigned Jupiter and, after the dress rehearsal, even suggested that "sovereign gods of Olympus" should have called him up as well. After thanking the Vienna Philharmonic for all its fine work, he declared that "maybe we will see each other again in a better world." The German late war effort had taken its toll on a composer who had hitherto refused to dwell in pessimism. A visibly distraught Strauss addressed the invited dress-rehearsal audience, lamenting that Western culture ("abendländische Kultur") in 1944 had finally come to an end, a public remark that would have led to the immediate arrest of most ordinary German citizens.

Even before scoring *Danae* Strauss was considering another theatrical project, one that he did not recognize as a full-fledged opera, but rather as an experimental stage piece for connoisseurs. Its roots go back to Stefan Zweig, who came upon an eighteenth-century libretto while working at the British Museum in 1934. The text, written by Giovanni Battista Casti (a rival to Lorenzo da Ponte), was a theatrical *divertimento* composed by Antonio Salieri and performed in the gardens of Schönbrunn in 1786 along with Mozart's *Der Schauspieldirektor*

(The Impresario). The Casti text, *Prima la musica, dopo le parole*, would ultimately become *Capriccio* (1941), subtitled "A Conversation Piece for Music." This extended one-act musical debate about words and music was intended neither for the regular opera house nor for the regular opera-going audience.

Instead, *Capriccio* was the culmination of a problem that had pre-occupied Strauss for decades: the dialectical relationship between *Ton* and *Wort* with all its attendant issues – textual audibility, modes of singing, the function of the orchestra, the role of dance and gesture. Over the decades Strauss had come far in his self-described struggle for balance between singers and the orchestra. If, for example, we compare his first and last one-act mythological operas – *Elektra* (1909) and *Daphne* (1938) – we see two operas that feature instrumental ensembles similar in size, but worlds apart in their sonic effects. *Daphne*, which emphasizes clarity, lyricism, transparency, is far removed from the turbulent sonic realm of *Elektra*. Important milestones along the way in this evolution include *Ariadne*, whose prologue intermingles spoken dialogue, recitative, and lyrical set numbers; *Intermezzo*, which continues this mixture, but in a more sophisticated way; and *Die schweigsame Frau*, Strauss's only opera to sustain a *parlante* style of singing for most of the work.

Though written during World War II, as Germany was about to mount its Russian campaign, *Capriccio* is set during a different type of conflict, during the so-called *Querelle des bouffons* (the "War of the Bouffons") of mid-eighteenth-century Paris, when – in a public dispute – the merits of French and Italian opera were hotly debated. The opera is rich both in historical allusions and in self-references: we hear quotations from Gluck, Piccinni, and Rameau; textual references to Metastasio, Pascal, and Ronsard; and self-borrowings from *Ariadne*, *Daphne*, and *Krämerspiegel*. Moreover, the characters are made up of allegorical figures: Flamand (music), Olivier (words), La Roche (stage direction), the Count and Countess (patrons). Strauss put Gregor to work on this Casti revival, but soon realized that such a unique, experimental work was simply beyond him. As with the per-

sonal, idiosyncratic *Intermezzo*, Strauss decided to write the text himself, though he ended up engaging the collaborative services of
Clemens Krauss as well. There is yet another name to be added to the
list of collaborators of Casti, Zweig, Gregor, Strauss, and Krauss –
namely the conductor Hans Swarovsky, who found the sixteenth-
century text (by Pierre de Ronsard of the *Pléiade*) for the sonnet around
which *Capriccio* turns.

Not unlike Wagner's *Meistersinger* Act III, where we witness the
genesis of Walther von Stolzing's *Preislied*, *Capriccio* also offers its
audience a view of the compositional process. First, the Count reads
the sonnet text alone; then it is read by its "author," Olivier, while
Flamand improvises at the harpsichord; and after the sonnet is composed, Flamand sings it to the Countess. The last of the thirteen
scenes marks the sonnet's final destination in its upward journey
from the prosaic baritonal declamation of the text to a musical setting
sung by a tenor, and finally to Strauss's favorite instrument – the
soprano voice. But before we reach the famous finale we must experience the pivotal ninth scene, a scene that reminds us of the work's
subtitle, "A Conversation Piece for Music." Scene nine, which is called
a fugue ("Discussion of the Theme: Words or Music."), is an animated
argument among the major characters. The centerpiece is La Roche's
monologue, where he (and, by extension, Strauss) asks:

> Where is the [modern] masterpiece that speaks to the hearts of
> people, in which their souls are reflected? Where is it? I cannot
> discover it, although I keep seaching. They make fun of the old and
> create nothing new.

An extended orchestral prelude (the so-called "moonlight music"
based on the eighth and last songs of *Krämerspiegel*) introduces the
final scene where the Countess must finally choose between the poet
and the composer. In order to make up her mind she sings through the
sonnet one last time. Whom will she choose? Strauss's final curtain
seems to leave the question open. Yet this final scene, one of the great
Straussian soprano monologues, radiates with some of Strauss's

finest composition, thereby suggesting strongly that music, not words, reigns supreme.

Reviews of the premiere were guarded, for the topic of this unique work flouted every official government requirement for war-time opera: it failed to glorify the image of the German *Volk*, it was hardly heroic, and the setting was pre-revolutionary Paris. What, indeed, are we to make of its apolitical stance? Can ignoring official dogma, itself, be interpreted as a political statement? Or is *Capriccio* an example of insensitivity on the part of the composer to contemporary issues, as certain post-war critics have argued? Should Strauss have been writing a work set in eighteenth-century France while Germany was mounting its Russian campaign? Such critics have offered more questions than satisfactory answers. What, in fact, should any composer – whether German, English, or Greek – have been writing in 1941? What, ultimately, is the role of a composer during any war? Without approaching the issue of politics and art on a broader, more contextualized level we are left with little more than "hortatory testimonials to the horror of German fascism, raised eyebrows and finger pointing."[1] One thing is certain: in a country where the National Socialists had politicized all aspects of German culture, Strauss himself saw *Capriccio* as a work outside the realm of politics.

Capriccio, completed on 3 August 1941, was the last work to receive an opus number. The 77-year-old Strauss declared his compositional career to be over, his next stage work would be "scored for harps," as he drolly put it. Undeterred by a composer who had already declared *Danae* to be his last opera, Clemens Krauss asked whether they might pursue yet another collaboration, to which Strauss replied: "Isn't this D♭ major [final scene] the best summation of my theatrical life's work? One can only leave one testament!"[2] D♭ major was, of course, a tonality of special significance for Strauss – the tonality of the sublime, the key of the final trio of *Der Rosenkavalier*. He chose this D♭ major trio for his funeral music in 1938, after hearing a broadcast of the opera under Knappertsbusch.

Following *Capriccio* Strauss stipulated that all new works were to be considered *Nachlass*, legacies for his family; moreover, his *Jugendwerke* were never to be published or performed in public. With typical Bavarian self-deprecating wit, he described the post-*Capriccio* compositions as mere *Handgelenksübungen*, musical "wrist exercises" to keep the hand in shape. These works, many of which are among his finest instrumental compositions, show a return to the classical genres of his youth: concerti, woodwind serenades, and lieder. Thus, in summer 1941 – after the completion of *Capriccio* – Strauss saw himself in a kind of exile, living in Garmisch with his family, cut off from the world, reading Goethe, writing memoirs and essays on music.

But political realities kept invading his world. Every time he thought he had reached an understanding concerning the safety of Alice and his two grandchildren, there arose new problems. Strauss still lived in fear of the upper echelon of the Nazi high command. Earlier in the year Strauss, along with Werner Egk and others, had gone to Berlin to discuss the issue of royalties from popular music versus classical music. As president of the Reichsmusikkammer, Strauss had ruled in 1934 that composers of so-called "serious music" (*ernste Musik*) should get a higher percentage. Goebbels had recently overruled that directive, and Strauss instructed a colleague that the Propaganda Minister had no right to interfere in affairs of composers. Egk described this meeting with Goebbels, where Strauss was brought first, receiving a tongue-lashing loud enough to be heard well beyond the closed doors:

> [Thereafer] we were all ushered in. Goebbels ordered that a letter that had been written by Strauss be read aloud: "As for the authorized statute [concerning royalties] we ourselves shall decide the questions of distribution. Goebbels has no right to interfere." Goebbels slapped at the letter and screamed: "Herr Strauss did you write that?" – "Yes" – "Silence! You have no idea who you are and who I am! You dare call Lehár a street musician?! I can feed this impertinence to the press . . . Lehár has the masses and you don't! . . . The art of tomorrow is different from the art of yesterday. You, Herr Strauss, are from yesterday!"[3]

Strauss left the meeting shaken and on the verge of tears. Fame and humiliation had become increasingly sharp juxtapositions for Strauss as the war progressed.

He now knew that he lacked any effective political leverage to protect his family. By September 1941, the only solution – as he saw it – was to move to Vienna. There family members could live under the protection of the Viennese Gauleiter, Baldur von Schirach, who was the son of a prominent theater Intendant who had grown up in a music-loving family. As Gauleiter, Schirach had ambitious cultural plans for Vienna, and he saw in Strauss someone who could possibly play a central role. On 1 September, they confirmed an arrangement obligating Strauss to do what he could for Viennese musical life, while his daughter-in-law and grandsons would be under his protection. The boys would not have to wear the Star of David while in public, and they would be able to receive the same education enjoyed by Aryans. Schirach had even received the blessing of Goebbels, who presented as a peace offering to Strauss for his seventy-seventh birthday a bust of Gluck by Houdon.[4]

For the meantime, things looked positive, secure, and settled. Strauss conducted operas and concerts in Vienna and received various honors (a silver medal from the Vienna Philharmonic and the commission of a bust to be placed in the State Opera). He also composed his first, and most famous, "wrist exercise": the Second Horn Concerto (1942). In his first real concerto since the First Horn Concerto of 1883, it is not difficult to imagine Strauss remembering the days when his father was still alive. What a different time was the world of 1883, the year of Wagner's death, the year the nineteen-year-old composer left the university for a winter in Berlin, and the year he first met Hans von Bülow. Sixty years later the city was now the target of allied bombing missions.

In March 1943 Munich sustained a severe air attack, while in Vienna air-raid drills had become routine. Strauss and his wife decided to return to Garmisch, but within days Pauline came down with a serious lung infection lasting some two months. Strauss was distressed, finding comfort only in composing his First Sonatina for Woodwinds ("From the Workshop of an Invalid"), another genre from his youth. By June 1943, Strauss felt his wife strong enough, and they left for their mountain villa in Garmisch, leaving Franz, Alice, and their two boys behind – all, ostensibly, still under the protection of Schirach. That August Strauss visited the Salzburg Festival, attending an *Arabella* under Krauss, and he conducted a Mozart concert, which would turn out to be his last public performance at the annual festival. There his new horn concerto was premiered by Gottfried von Freiberg under the baton of the young Karl Böhm.

Things took a dramatic turn for the worse when, on the night of 2 October, the Munich Opera was destroyed by aerial bombing. "I am beside myself," Strauss wrote his sister, Johanna, the next day. This was the very theater where he had heard his first opera, where his father had played first horn; it was also the house that had seen the premieres of *Rheingold*, *Walküre*, *Tristan*, and *Meistersinger*, as well as Strauss's *Friedenstag* and *Capriccio*. Worse yet, on 6 October Strauss, alone at home, was visited by the Kreisleiter from Garmisch, who informed him that his nineteen-room villa would be used to house evacuees and other homeless victims of the war. It was his heroic duty for the home front, Kreisleiter Windsheim insisted, to which Strauss replied: "No soldier need fight on my account." Windsheim followed with an open threat: "In recent days more important heads than yours have rolled."[5] Strauss was unnerved.

Two days later, Hans Frank, Governor-General of Poland, telephoned, saying that he was in Munich and would like to visit for tea. Frank, who had admired Strauss's music since he was a boy, saw an opportunity to meet the great composer, Strauss saw the opportunity to possibly reverse a directive from the Kreisleiter. Frank promised to speak with Windsheim upon his departure, and within a month the villa was spared. But that was hardly the end of the affair. Strauss's remarks about German soldiers and his refusal to refer to Hitler as the Führer had gotten as high as the office of Martin Bormann (the Nazi

17   The Munich Opera in ruins following an allied attack in 1943

Party Chancellor and Hitler's deputy), who sent out a directive to reverse the recent decision.

Strauss sent a letter directly to Hitler, reminding him that Frank had already declared his house off-limits:

> The villa is filled with valuable artworks, my own musical manuscripts and memoirs of a half century and the complicated business of running the house (especially while we are away in Vienna) cannot be entrusted to strangers.[6]

Hitler ultimately gave in, by turning the decision over to the local council, but not before Bormann sent out another directive on 24 January that all party officials were to end all "personal dealings" with Strauss.

As painful as all this domestic uncertainty must have been, it was nonetheless far more benign than what took place that winter, an incident that exposed the limits of Schirach's protection. One evening in January 1943, Franz and Alice were playing cards at the house of some friends in Vienna when eight Gestapo agents entered, around 10:30, asking whether they were listening to a foreign radio broadcast. After inspecting the radio, the agents left. Later that night at approximately 2:00 a.m. the Gestapo entered the Strauss home on Jacquingasse, arresting both Franz and Alice, leaving behind their sons Richard and Christian, ages seventeen and twelve respectively. Despite the state of panic and confusion, Franz was able to instruct the elder Richard to get in touch with a family friend, Manfred Mautner Markhof, who notified Karl Böhm, who – in turn – contacted Schirach's assistant, Walter Thomas. After two days the composer's son and daughter were released from their incarceration at the Hotel Metropol (party head-quarters in Vienna), though no reason was ever given for their arrest.[7]

Alice Strauss was, of course, lucky to be alive. Her mother had escaped earlier to Lucerne; her grandmother, along with Alice's other siblings, was left behind in Prague. Usually reluctant to speak of pain-ful wartime memories, Alice, in a rare moment, once recalled to a family friend:

> We knew that many members of my family had been taken to Theresienstadt and we thought there must be a labor camp there, where they were collecting Jewish people before resettling them somewhere. We knew nothing of the extermination, and wouldn't have believed it. Now and then we received postcards with a few words of greeting. My old grandmother [Paula Neumann] died there – we heard about that.
>
> During the war Papa [Strauss] traveled from Vienna to Dresden. He stopped in Theresienstadt and wanted to visit my grandmother. He went to the camp-gate and said: "My name is Richard Strauss, I want to see Frau Neumann." The SS guards thought he was a lunatic and sent him packing.[8]

After Paula Neumann died all that Alice received was a small portrait, some clothing, and an official document stating that she died of "spot-ted fever." All in all, twenty-six of Alice Strauss's relatives perished in Theresienstadt, Auschwitz, and other camps. Once again, composi-tion was Strauss's only solace during this dreadful period of late 1943 and early 1944, when he began sketching a Second Sonatina for Woodwinds, curiously bearing the subtitle "The Happy Workshop."

The year 1944 (particularly the month of June, the composer's eightieth birthday) was supposed to be one of celebration, but in the light of Strauss's recent behavior and Bormann's angry reaction, the Nazis seriously considered banning any public celebration at all. In a letter (26 April 1944) to Goebbels, Wilhelm Furtwängler wrote a strong letter of support: "Richard Strauss is, for any serious musician, the greatest living composer today, not only in Germany but in the entire musical world (thus, also in France, England, America, Japan, etc.)." He argued that a composer with such international profile would only become a martyr in the eyes of the allies and that it would indeed be embarrassing for Germany's best living composer to be boycotted in his own land.[9] Shortly thereafter a compromise was worked out that permitted a celebration – in public and over the airwaves – of the music of Strauss, but not the man.

In Vienna, where Baldur von Schirach still enjoyed significant autonomy, an extensive two-week birthday festival was to celebrate Strauss and his music beginning on 1 June, but with the provision that the composer would receive no certificates, awards, or other personal honors. The first six evenings saw performances of *Ariadne auf Naxos*, *Der Rosenkavalier*, *Capriccio*, and *Arabella*. On the day of his birthday, 11 June, a special noonday concert was given, opening with the *Meistersinger* prelude under Böhm, who then presented the composer with a special baton of ebony, ivory, and silver. Strauss took the heavy stick and conducted *Till Eulenspiegel*, thereafter exchanging it for his own lighter baton in order to lead the Vienna Philharmonic in *Symphonia domestica*, smiling to his wife and son, as their themes were played by the orchestra. At six that evening, Böhm conducted *Ariadne* (broadcast live over the radio), which was followed by a gala dinner for invited guests. There were various tributes, including a festival lecture given by Joseph Gregor, his former librettist. Other orchestral concerts followed, as well as evenings of lieder and chamber music; during this fortnight Strauss also recorded all his major tone poems with the Vienna Philharmonic. If Strauss thought this semi-official recognition in Vienna extended to Berlin, he was sorely mistaken, for just one day after the festival his application for a tourist visa to Switzerland was denied.

After the production of *Danae* fell through, following Goebbel's declaration of total war, Strauss wrote Franz and Alice that "sorrow, worry, harrassment, and panic" had him near the breaking point. He would get through the days making musical arrangements (such as a new *Rosenkavalier* suite), copying out new scores of old tone poems, and doing intensive reading: Wagner's essays, Homer, Nestroy, Shakespeare, Dickens, Plutarch, and especially Goethe. But outside his Garmisch villa the situation worsened: allied bombing raids increased, Munich was in flames, Strauss's birthplace (on Altheimer Eck) was destroyed, and Vienna was becoming even more dangerous. Strauss urged Franz, Alice, and the grandchildren to come to Garmisch, and by December all were together except for young Richard, who was required to work in a factory outside Vienna. At the end of the month the Strauss villa on Jacquingasse was seriously damaged.

In the meantime Strauss was sketching a tribute to his beloved Munich, now in ruins ("a Bavarian Pompeii," Strauss sardonically observed). This tribute dates back to 1938, when Strauss was asked to compose music for a documentary film on Munich. Musical material for the film had been drawn from *Feuersnot*, a fitting idea since the opera was set in the medieval city. The Nazis ultimately forbade the film's release, but Strauss published the music under the title *München: Ein Gelegenheitswalzer* (1939). After the bombings, this five-minute "occasional waltz" was expanded, with an ominous middle section (taken from the part in *Feuersnot* when Munich is shrouded in darkness), and given a new subtitle, *Ein Gedächtniswalzer* ("Memorial Waltz").

But Strauss was also at work on a far more serious project, inspired by a commission from Paul Sacher in August 1944. By far the most profound instrumental work of this late period, a work with a sustained seriousness of purpose not seen since *Death and Transfiguration*, Strauss's *Metamorphosen* bears the subtitle "A Study for Twenty-Three

Strings." It was based on a poem by Goethe, "Niemand wird sich selber kennen" (No one can know himself):

> No one can know himself
> separate from his inner being,
> Yet he tries to do it every day,
> That which is clearly from the outside,
> What he is and what he was,
> What he can do and what he wants to do.
>
> But what happens in the world,
> No one actually understands,
> And up to the present day,
> No one wishes to understand,
> Conduct yourself with reason,
> As the day is at hand,
> Always think: "It's gone all right until now,
> So it may well continue that way until the end."

In a rare moment of self-revelation, Strauss composed a work of compelling depth and profundity, a work that seeks to probe the cause of war itself, which is an act that steps from mankind's bestial nature. In short, Strauss inverts the classical metamorphosis (where through self-knowledge Man becomes divine), realizing instead humanity's dangerous potential toward the basest animal instincts.[10] In this context, the Beethoven *Eroica* funeral-march quotation, which emerges in a seemingly inevitable way toward the end, is painfully ironic. It represents the fate of German culture, which – as Strauss later observed in a short memorandum – had come to an end:

> From 1 May onwards the most terrible period of human history came
> to an end, the twelve-year reign of bestiality, ignorance, and anti-
> culture under the greatest criminals, during which Germany's 2,000
> years of cultural evolution met its doom and irreplaceable
> monuments of architecture and works of art were destroyed by a
> criminal soldiery.[11]

Physical reminders of cultural demise were becoming ever more frequent: on 3 February the Lindenoper in Berlin was destroyed, the

Dresden Opera ten days later, and on 12 March the Vienna State Opera was completely destroyed except for the outer walls. All three cities had played such a vital role in Strauss's life: in Berlin he had achieved world fame from 1898 to 1918; in Dresden nine of his fifteen operas received their world premieres; and in Vienna, his second home, he had directed the State Opera from 1919 to 1924.

Three days after the Vienna Opera was destroyed Strauss received a telegram from the Bavarian State Ministry, warning that Alice would be arrested and sent to a camp in the foreseeable future. Her life was spared both by an influential friend in the ministry (who succeeded in delaying her papers) and by the war's end in early May. American soldiers were in Garmisch by 30 April, the day of Hitler's suicide, and the larger villas were taken over by the occupying troops for the quartering of troops. It appeared that Strauss's home would be no exception as the composer went to his front gate, declaring: "I am Richard Strauss, the composer of *Der Rosenkavalier* and *Salome*." As luck would have it, the American officer in the jeep was fond of Strauss's music and immediately declared the composer's villa "off limits," and a grateful Strauss invited the soldiers in for food and wine. The celebrity-composer received many visits from American soldiers, whom Strauss found to be "extremely kind and friendly ... I can hardly get away from the autograph-hunters – many's the time I have to note down the waltz from *Rosenkavalier*, and, on one occasion, the Don Juan motif."

One of those military visitors was a 24-year-old musician named John de Lancie, who had been an oboist with the Pittsburgh Symphony Orchestra before military service. He visited Strauss accompanied by the German-born American musicologist Alfred Mann, who acted partly as an interpreter during the conversation. The shy, young de Lancie – who later had a distinguished career with the Philadelphia Orchestra – observed that some of Strauss's finest melodies were written for oboe, and he asked whether he had thought of writing a work for the instrument. The taciturn composer simply replied, "No," and that was the end of it – or so de Lancie thought. Strauss, however, soon began work on an oboe concerto, which he finished, in full score, by mid October, to be premiered in February 1946.

The performance took place in Switzerland, where Strauss and his wife had moved in October. With food and fuel shortages, the coming winter looked grim for the elderly composer and his wife. Moreover, there was no stabilized currency, and Strauss's accounts and future royalties had been frozen until further notice. Because of his official connection with the National Socialist government in the early 1930s, he would go through a de-Nazification hearing, but *in absentia*. Their first stop, once across the Swiss border, was Baden near Zurich, where they stayed in a hotel and were befriended by Swiss music critic and future biographer Willi Schuh. The sale of sketchbooks and manuscripts provided loans and some income during this period, when the composer's health declined steadily. Strauss occasionally visited the Schuh home in Zurich, though one particular visit caused the composer great pain. It was an evening when Schuh showed Strauss a copy of Alma Mahler's *Gustav Mahler: Memories and Letters* (1940). Strauss was incredulous at the erroneous, venomous distortions in the text, reading the book in a single sitting, well into the early morning. Not only had she made unflattering remarks about Strauss (and especially his wife) but she had suppressed how helpful Strauss had been for Mahler's early career. As president of the Allgemeiner deutscher Musikverein, Strauss had arranged three important performances of Mahler symphonies, two of which were premieres: no. 3 in Krefeld (1902) and no. 6 in Essen (1906). In Berlin, Strauss programmed the first performance of the then incomplete Second Symphony in 1895 and the premiere of Mahler's Fourth for Berlin in 1901. In each case, he yielded the baton to Mahler, although he undertook many preliminary rehearsals.

Alma Mahler-Werfel noted these very performances in her book, but without any mention of Strauss, who angrily filled the margins of Schuh's volume with copious annotations. What hurt him most of all were the comments concerning his wife: "The inventions, distortions, and lies about a faithful and decent woman in this sorry work will inevitably pass judgment on the work itself. My wife had been warned by many Viennese, even by Ludwig Karpath, not to associate with Mahler's widow." Strauss was equally dismayed by passages in Mahler's letters to Alma in which opinions of Strauss ranged from admiration to expressions of Mahler's artistic superiority. Atop the title page of the book Strauss summarized his opinion of the entire volume: "Amateurish, incorrectly recorded inferiority complexes."[12] Sadly, Mahler-Werfel's inaccuracies served as a source of misinformation about the relationship between Mahler and Strauss that was not rectified until the 1980s.[13]

One highlight of his stay in Zurich was the premiere of the *Metamorphosen* on 25 January 1946, conducted by Paul Sacher, who had commissioned the work. Strauss declined his invitation to attend, but did visit the final rehearsal, asking Sacher whether he could conduct the work himself. It is telling that with this work of rare self-expression, the composer could not bear the thought of being surrounded by a large audience. Such was not the case with the Oboe Concerto a month later, performed by Marcel Saillet under Volkmar Andreae leading the Zurich Tonhalle Orchestra. Strauss not only attended the concert (which also included his "Potpourri" from *Die schweigsame Frau*) but was the guest of honor at a small celebration later that evening.

His thoughts soon returned to composing, having accepted an offer to write a children's opera for the school his grandson, Christian, was attending. It was to be based on a work by Wieland to be called *Des Esels Schatten* (The Donkey's Shadow), with a libretto constructed by Hans Adler, but Strauss never finished it beyond fair sketches. The incomplete little *Schuloper* was orchestrated and expanded by Karl Haussner, who conducted it at the school to celebrate the hundredth anniversary of Strauss's birth. Another project came to fruition, however, the delightful *Duett-Concertino*, a work for clarinet, bassoon, and string orchestra, probably based on Hans Christian Andersen's *The Princess and the Swineherd*. Strauss was too ill to attend the premiere in April 1948.

The nomadic hotel life was taking its toll on the elderly couple, who briefly considered an invitation from Lionel Barrymore – a life-long admirer of Strauss's music – to come to Hollywood and live as his guests. But leaving Europe and their family was out of the question, and in 1947 they spent winter in Baden, spring in Lugano, summer in Pontresina, and fall in Montreux and Zurich. The main event that autumn was a London concert tour that had been arranged by Strauss's publisher, Ernst Roth. It was not an easy trip for the somewhat frail 83-year-old composer, who traveled by airplane for the first time in his life, but the Strauss Festival would offer income and provide diversion for an old man who was now living in relative isolation.

Strauss arrived in London on the afternoon of 4 October; the opening concert on the next evening featured the Royal Philharmonic under Sir Thomas Beecham, who conducted the suite from *Der Bürger als Edelmann*, the love-scene from *Feuersnot*, and *Don Quixote* (with Paul Tortelier as solo 'cellist), and the young Norman del Mar conducted the recently arranged Symphonic Fantasy from *Die Frau ohne Schatten*. Because Pauline stayed behind, Willi Schuh served as the composer's traveling companion for much of the festival, as did Roth and Maria Cebotari, the soprano who had premiered the role of Daphne in 1938.

The trip offered not only musical opportunities, but the chance for Strauss to revisit his favorite museums: the National Gallery and the Wallace Collection. The main public event was slated for 19 October, when Strauss conducted the Philharmonia Orchestra in the Royal Albert Hall to an audience of 7,500. The composer began with "God Save the King" and conducted *Don Juan*, the *Burleske* (with Alfred Blumen as solo pianist), the *Symphonia domestica*, and his new arrangement of the *Rosenkavalier* waltzes as an encore. Hofmannsthal's widow, Gerty, and Elisabeth Schumann paid a visit during the intermission. Another festival highlight included a BBC broadcast concert of *Elektra* under Beecham.

Back in Montreux, Strauss, whose life-long instinct was to wave off pessimism, found it increasingly difficult to put a positive face on much of anything. His days were spent corresponding with cultural officials, writing artistic testaments for the reactivation of European culture. It distressed Franz to see his father – obsessed with events well beyond his control – spend the end of his life writing pointless letters. He thus encouraged him to give up the letter writing and return to composing, suggesting he might return to lieder composition. As annoyed as Strauss was by his son's suggestion, he knew that Franz was ultimately right. Two years earlier, while in Ouchy, Strauss jotted his first sketches of Im Abendrot, a poem by Eichendorff, but broke off composition, and Franz's advice may well have, in part, reawakened that lyrical impulse of 1946 for in 1948 he began composing these songs quite steadily.

Im Abendrot (completed in May 1948) would be the first of four orchestral songs that were performed and published posthumously under the title Vier letzte Lieder (Four Last Songs), a title invented by Ernst Roth, Strauss's English publisher (Boosey and Hawkes), who also devised the order in which they are commonly performed. We can never know in what order Strauss would have put them, or whether he even intended them as a complete set, although this seems likely. After he scored the last song on 20 September 1948, he handed them to Alice and with deliberate – if not mock – abruptness stated, "Here are the songs your husband ordered."[14] The other three songs in this group are settings of poems by Hermann Hesse: Frühling (Spring), Beim Schlafengehen (Going to Sleep), and September, completed in July, August, and September 1948, respectively. According to Strauss's wish, Kirsten Flagstad premiered these songs (in London) under Wilhelm Furtwängler.

Around the time he was composing Im Abendrot, Strauss orchestrated a song from his Op. 27 collection of lieder he had written for Pauline, to celebrate their wedding. Although composed in 1894, this song, "Ruhe, meine Seele!", takes on new meaning after the Second World War. The poem addresses the fundamental tension between peace and conflict, opposing states that are as much a simultaneous phenomenon as they are juxtaposed. For the peace described in the poem is unnatural, it is forced, much like the artificial night-time created by the cover of foliage blotting out the sun mentioned in the opening: "Through the leaves a dark veil steals the bright sunshine." The stillness described by Karl Henckell's text is a turbulent, volatile one, much like the eye of a hurricane; rather than confront turmoil, the poem urges us to "forget what threatens you." Indeed, as we read the poem the troubled character has already made that decision, and the line, "your storms were wild" tells how furious the turmoil once was. The poet's solution is not to confront that turbulence, to work out those things that troubled the soul, but simply to forget. It has been suggested that this song, which seems to reflect Strauss's state of mind with the upheaval of war and its aftermath, may well have been intended to be included with the four other songs.[15]

Whatever the case may be, at the end of his life, we see Strauss – much like Mahler in *Das Lied von der Erde* – turning to the genre of orchestral song, setting poems that contemplate the meaning of death through nature. In his sequence for these songs, Roth pairs two works that pertain to the change of seasons: *Frühling* celebrates the sound, sight, and fragrance of spring; *September* looks at the change from summer to autumn, as the garden comes to its yearly end. The second pair concerns the desire to sleep. "Now the day has made me tired," the soprano sings in *Beim Schlafengehen*, "All my senses want to sink in slumber." *Im Abendrot*, which presents a silent landscape on the verge of night, brings us to the end of our journey: "How tired we are from wandering, could this perhaps be death?" That final word brings us back to the world of *Death and Transfiguration*, with the famous theme of the "Ideal" in the English horn. These luminescent, autumnal songs are among Strauss's finest works in any genre.

In 1948 Strauss was cleared by the de-Nazification tribunal in Munich, though he was in great physical pain, suffering from a bladder stone which was removed at the Clinique Cécil in Lausanne in December of that year. He convalesced for weeks, reading the scores of Beethoven, Wagner, and Haydn while in bed. After seven weeks of hospitalization he and his wife left for Montreux, where they stayed for several months until Strauss had the strength to return home to Garmisch. On 10 May Willi Schuh and other friends bade the Strausses farewell. Within a month, Strauss would be celebrating his eighty-fifth birthday, honored by the world. Bayreuth bestowed honorary citizenship on 8 June, and two days later he went to Munich to attend part of a dress rehearsal of *Der Rosenkavalier*, under Georg Solti – Strauss himself conducted the very end of Act II for a film-biography entitled "A Life for Music." The film shows an aged composer conducting the famous waltz of Baron Ochs, using his left hand only to turn pages of the score, cueing the singers with his eyes. It was the last time he would conduct in public.

At his birthday ceremony in Garmisch the next day, attended by the Bavarian president, the cultural minister, and the mayors of Munich and Garmisch, Strauss received an honorary doctorate from the University of Munich School of Law and honorary citizenship from Garmisch. That evening Eugen Papst conducted a Strauss concert with the Munich Philharmonic. The composer returned to Munich a month later to conduct the "moonlight music" from *Capriccio* at the Bavarian Radio studio for his film biography; it was the last thing he ever conducted. A month later he suffered a mild heart attack and was confined to his bed in Garmisch.

One of the last friends to visit him was Rudolf Hartmann, the stage director who had produced the premieres of *Friedenstag*, *Capriccio*, and *Die Liebe der Danae*. He was also teaching stage direction to Strauss's grandson, Richard. The visit took place on 30 August, and by then Strauss knew he was going to die. But before he did, he was determind to insure that a younger generation would help rebuild and resurrect the opera houses of Vienna, Dresden, and Munich. He saw Hartmann as his messenger. "There is so much I would still have to do," Strauss told Hartmann, "but I believe that some of what I wanted and have begun has fallen on fertile ground."[16] At the end of their conversation, Strauss recalled a line from *Tristan*: "Grüss mir die Welt," the moment when Isolde has resolved that she must die and asks Brangäne to be her messenger, to give the world her final greeting.

After Hartmann departed, Strauss was exhausted but serene, telling Alice that "I can now die in peace, all artistic questions have been discussed, [Hartmann] can lay everything out for [Franz]." On 6 September, his fever had reached an alarming level, and he was sliding in and out of consciousness. Alice, with the devotion of a daughter, stayed by his side, recording much of what he said in his feverish state:

> I am not afraid to die, Hartmann knows what must be done . . . What I now experience I could compose entirely, I wrote it sixty years ago, it was exactly like that [in *Death and Transfiguration*].[17]

Two days later he went into a coma, breathing irregularly, and at 2:12 in the afternoon he died from renal failure. A death mask was made, and according to Strauss's wishes, he was cremated.

An 11:00 a.m. memorial service was held at the Ostfriedhof in Munich on an unseasonably warm and humid 12 September; a heady floral fragrance from the countless flower arrangements permeated the air. The Bavarian president, the mayor of Munich, and other dignitaries were in attendance, including Georg Solti, who led the Munich Philharmonic with the funeral march from Beethoven's *Eroica* and, following Strauss's request, the final trio from *Der Rosenkavalier*. The singers (Marianne Schech, Maud Cunitz, and Gerda Sommerschuh) were so overcome with emotion that, one by one, they dropped out – with Solti continuing to conduct the orchestra – and slowly they came back in the end. Pauline, herself ill and overcome with grief, fell to her knees, crying out for her departed husband. She would survive him by only eight months.

Agnostic to the end, Strauss – with dignity and without a hint of self-pity – affirmed that he was not afraid to die, that he had lived a full life. To those loved ones surrounding his bed he maintained: "I have done my job, there is nothing more to do." These may well have been his last words. Even with the knowledge of approaching death, he neither needed nor wanted redemption, continuing to hold to his life-

18 Strauss in June 1949, three months before his death

long belief that the divine is to be found on earth: in art, in ideas, in the act of creation. In the days before his death, Strauss spoke often about the notion of immortality: "When he died," the composer remarked to the attending physician standing at his bedside, "Goethe was never so alive and renowned as he is today." Today, a half century after his death, the same can be said of Richard Strauss.

Introduction

1 See Chapter 2, pp. 57–58.
2 Richard Strauss, "Letzte Aufzeichnung," of June 1949, *Betrachtungen und Erinnerungen*, ed. Willi Schuh, 2nd edn. (Zurich: Atlantis, 1957), p. 182. Thus, by the last decade of the nineteenth century, Strauss was fully aware of an eroding relationship that Adorno would later refer to as the dichotomy of "subject" and "object," a predicament of modernism that Adorno claimed Strauss did not understand.

1 Musical development and early career

1 A life-long devotee of the natural horn, Franz Strauss maintained that Wagner's horn parts were designed for the clarinet.
2 Letter by Strauss to Ludwig Thuille (31 December 1877), in *Richard Strauss and his World*, ed. Bryan Gilliam (Princeton, NJ: Princeton University Press, 1992), p. 198.
3 Letter by Strauss to Thuille (28 October 1878), *Richard Strauss and His World*, p. 212.
4 Wagner's title sounds almost like 'Lohengrün,' or 'Lohengreen.'
5 *Richard Strauss and his World*, p. 227.
6 Willi Schuh, *Richard Strauss: A Chronicle of the Early Years 1864–1898*, trans. Mary Whittall (Cambridge: Cambridge University Press, 1982), p. 49.
7 *Richard Strauss: Briefe an die Eltern*, ed. Willi Schuh (Zurich: Atlantis, 1954), p. 32.

8   *Briefe an die Eltern*, p. 39.

9   Richard Strauss, *Recollections and Reflections*, ed. Willi Schuh, trans. L. J. Lawrence (London: Boosey and Hawkes, 1953), p. 119.

10 *Gustav Mahler/Richard Strauss: Correspondence, 1888–1911*, ed. Herta Blaukopf, trans. Edmund Jephcott (Chicago: University of Chicago Press, 1984), p. 106.

11 Schuh, *Chronicle*, p. 84.

12 "Memories of Mahler," *Klemperer on Music: Shavings from a Musician's Workbench*, ed. Martin Anderson (Exeter: Toccata Press, 1986), p. 148.

2   *"Onward and away to ever-new victories"*: Strauss's emergence as a tone poet

1   *Recollections and Reflections*, p. 120.

2   Schuh, *Chronicle*, p. 99.

3   *Briefe an die Eltern*, p. 65.

4   *Recollections and Reflections*, pp. 138–39.

5   *Hans von Bülow and Richard Strauss: Correspondence*, ed. Willi Schuh and Franz Trenner, trans. Anthony Gishford (London: Boosey and Hawkes, 1955), p. 24.

6   Ibid., p. 34.

7   Ibid., pp. 82–83.

8   Letter of 12 October 1889, *Cosima Wagner – Richard Strauss: Ein Briefwechsel*, ed. Franz Trenner (Tutzing: Hans Schneider, 1978), p. 8.

9   Letter of 25 February 1890, ibid., p. 26.

10 Letter of 22 March 1890, ibid., p. 35.

11 Charles Youmans, "Richard Strauss's *Guntram* and the Dismantling of Wagnerian Musical Metaphysics" (Ph.D. Diss. Duke University, 1996), p. iv.

12 *C. Wagner–Strauss Briefwechsel*, p. 227.

13 Willi Schuh, "Der Sohn im Wort und in der Musik des Vaters," *Festschrift Dr. Franz Strauss* (Tutzing: Hans Schneider, 1967), p. 104. Richard's son Franz was born just four days earlier.

14 Louis's remarks about Strauss's tone poems appear in English translation in *Richard Strauss and His World*, pp. 305–10.

15 This section, "the hero's adversaries," is perhaps the least understood, possibly owing to Willi Schuh's misreading of Strauss's sketchbook annotations where the composer writes that the hero "arises in order to confront the inner enemies (doubt, disgust) and

external enemies." The word order (first inner, then outer) is not accidental, for "disgust" is Zarathustra's primary nemesis, and in a later symphonic project (*Künstlertragödie*) – that ultimately became *Eine Alpensinfonie* – an artist likewise struggles with resignation and self-doubt.

3   The rise of an opera composer

1 Letter to Pauline, 4 December 1901, Richard Strauss Archive – Garmisch (henceforth, RSA).

2 *Briefe an die Eltern*, p. 272.

3 We recall from the second chapter that the young Rösch, himself a composer, was alarmed in the early 1890s when Strauss rejected Schopenhauer and musical metaphysics. What an ironic twist that he later became a lawyer whose principal expertise had to do with music as a commodity.

4 Strauss's substantial, quarter-hour setting of Dehmel's *Notturno* (1899) could have been a model for any number of Strauss's future operatic monologues, especially the one by Salome just six years later.

5 Schuh, *Chronicle*, pp. 310 and 312f.

6 Letter to Pauline, 2 September 1901, RSA.

7 Letter to Pauline, 20 October 1902, RSA.

8 Letter of 5 July 1905, *Richard Strauss and Romain Rolland: Correspondence, Diary, Essays*, ed. and trans. Rollo Myers (Berkeley, CA: University of California Press, 1968), p. 29.

9 Leon Botstein, "The Enigmas of Strauss: A Revisionist View," *Richard Strauss and His World*, p. 22.

10 Quoted in Hermann Unger, *Lebendige Musik in Zwei Jahrtausende* (Cologne, 1940), p. 305.

11 *Strauss–Rolland Correspondence*, p. 82.

12 Theodor W. Adorno, "Social Character," *In Search of Wagner*, trans. Rodney Livingstone (London: Verso, 1991), p. 17.

13 *A Working Friendship: The Correspondence between Richard Strauss and Hugo von Hofmannsthal*, ed. Willi Schuh, trans. Hanns Hammelmann and Ewald Osers (Cambridge: Cambridge University Press, 1980), p. 27.

14 *Ibid.*, p. 29.

15 Hofmannsthal, letter to Countess Ottonie von Degenfeld (24 January
    1911). Transcript in Willi Schuh Nachlass.

16 Richard Strauss, *Schreibkalender* 1911, RSA.

17 Hugo von Hofmannsthal, "Letter of Lord Chandos," *Selected Prose*,
    trans. Mary Hottinger and Tania and James Stern, Bollingen Series
    33, no. 1 (New York: Bollingen Foundation, 1952), pp. 140–41.

18 Letter to Strauss (4 November 1911), *Strauss–Hofmannsthal
    Correspondence*, p. 105.

19 *Strauss–Hofmannsthal Correspondence*, p. 94.

20 Letter to Hofmannsthal (February 1915), ibid., p. 216.

21 Letter to Gerty von Hofmannsthal (31 July 1914), Michael Kennedy,
    Richard Strauss, 2nd edn. (London: J. M. Dent, 1988), p. 58.

4 *Between two empires: Strauss in the 1920s*

1 *Strauss–Hofmannsthal Correspondence*, p. 307.

2 Letter of 17 June 1922, *Richard Strauss – Franz Schalk: Ein Briefwechsel*,
   ed. Günter Brosche (Tutzing: Hans Schneider, 1983), pp. 199–200.

3 Letter of 22 June 1922, *Strauss–Schalk Briefwechsel*, p. 205. We recall
   from the previous chapter that Strauss's plan for financial
   independence by age fifty had been thwarted after the British
   government confiscated his savings that had been put in their banks.

4 The inevitable quote from *Death and Transfiguration* is one of many
   humorous self-quotations.

5 *Strauss–Rolland Correspondence*, p. 165.

6 *Strauss–Hofmannsthal Correspondence*, pp. 248–49.

7 Ibid., p. 249.

8 From a letter by Hartlaub to Alfred H. Barr (8 July 1929), who quoted
   it in "Otto Dix," *The Arts* 17 (1931), p. 237.

9 "Arnold Schoenberg an Anton Webern: Eine Auswahl unbekannter
   Briefe," *Arnold Schoenberg Gedenkaustellung 1974*, ed. Ernst Hillmar
   (Vienna: Universal, 1974), pp. 47–48.

10 Heinrich Kralik in the *Neues Wiener Tagblatt* (3 November 1924).

11 *Strauss–Hofmannsthal Correspondence*, p. 350.

12 The above is a paraphrase by Gordon Craig, *The Germans* (New York:
    Putnam, 1982), p. 33. See also Troeltsch's essay, "The German
    Democracy," translated in *The Weimar Sourcebook*, ed. Anton Kaes,

Martin Jay, and Edward Dimenberg (Berkeley, CA: University of California Press, 1994), pp. 89–91.

13 Gerhard Splitt, *Richard Strauss 1933–1935: Ästhetik und Musikpolitik zu Beginn der nationalsozialistischen Herrschaft* (Pfaffenweiller: Centaurus, 1987), p. 50.

14 *Strauss–Hofmannsthal Correspondence*, p. 364.

5 After Hofmannsthal: personal and political crises

1 Michael Meyer, in *The Politics of Music in the Third Reich* (New York: Peter Lang, 1991), is the most recent of many commentators who have either asserted or implied erroneously that Strauss wrote the *Olympic Hymn* as a concession to glorify the Nazi government (see p. 194).

2 Strauss, "The History of *Die schweigsame Frau*," *A Confidential Matter: The Letters of Richard Strauss and Stefan Zweig, 1931–1935*, ed. Willi Schuh, trans. Max Knight (Berkeley, CA: University of California Press, 1977), pp. 107–10.

3 *Strauss–Zweig Letters*, p. 29.

4 Ibid., pp. 99–100.

5 Michael Kater, *The Twisted Muse* (New York: Oxford University Press, 1997), p. 209.

6 Joseph Gregor, *Richard Strauss: Der Meister der Oper* (Munich: Piper, 1939), pp. 246–47.

7 "Friede im Innern," translation by Susan Gillespie.

8 "Sühnung," translation by Susan Gillespie.

9 Norma Del Mar, *Richard Strauss: A Critical Commentary on His Life and Works*. 2nd edn., 3 vols. (Ithaca, NY: Cornell University Press, 1986), vol. III, p. 111.

10 "Selections from the Strauss–Gregor Correspondence" in *Richard Strauss and His World*, pp. 267–68.

11 See Dagmar Wünsche, "Richard Strauss – Heinz Tietjen: Briefe der Freundschaft" in *Richard Strauss-Blätter* 20 (Dec. 1988), p. 112.

12 Letter to Tietjen (7 March 1939) in "Briefe der Freundschaft," p. 118.

13 From the memoirs of Otto Strasser, member of the Vienna Philharmonic: *Und dafür wird man noch bezahlt* (Vienna: Paul Neff, 1974), p. 182.

6 "Now the day has made me tired": the War and its aftermath

1 See Edward Said's review of the 1992 Bard College Music Festival, "Music," in The Nation (25 January 1993), p. 101.

2 Willi Schuh, Über Opern von Richard Strauss (Zurich: Atlantis, 1947), p. 101.

3 Werner Egk, Die Zeit wartet nicht (Munich: Goldmann, 1981), p. 978.

4 Worried that the bust might have been stolen, Strauss inquired about its provenance shortly after the war and discovered that it had, indeed, been legitimately purchased by the German government at a fair price.

5 "Bericht über neuerliche Belästung von Dr. Richard Strauss und seiner Familie seitens der Kreisleitung," n.d., RSA.

6 Letter of 16 January 1944, Berlin Document Center.

7 Personal communication with Christian Strauss, August 1996, Santa Fe, New Mexico.

8 Kurt Wilhelm, Richard Strauss: An Intimate Portrait, trans. Mary Whittall (London: Thames and Hudson, 1989), p. 264.

9 Letter in the Berlin Document Center.

10 See Timothy L. Jackson, "The Metamorphosis of the Metamorphosen," Richard Strauss: New Perspectives on the Composer and his Work, ed. Bryan Gilliam (Durham, NC: Duke University Press, 1992), p. 195.

11 RSA.

12 From a transcript made by Alice Strauss (1948) in the RSA.

13 The first major work in the area was Gustav Mahler/Richard Strauss: Correspondence, 1888–1911, ed. Herta Blaukopf, trans. Edmund Jephcott (Chicago: University of Chicago Press, 1984).

14 Personal communication from Christian Strauss, July 1997, Garmisch.

15 Timothy L. Jackson, "Ruhe, meine Seele! and the Letzte Orchesterlieder," Richard Strauss and His World, pp. 90–137.

16 Rudolf Hartmann, "The Last Visit with Strauss," Richard Strauss and His World, pp. 298–99.

17 The composer's words were recorded by Alice Strauss, who sat at his bedside. See her "Aufzeichnungen der Fieberphantasie von Dr. Richard Strauss aus 6. September 1949" ("Notes from the fever-delirium of Dr. Richard Strauss from 6 September 1949"), RSA.

SELECTED FURTHER READING

Correspondence

Hans von Bülow and Richard Strauss: Correspondence. Ed. Willi Schuh and
 Franz Trenner. Trans. Anthony Gishford. London: Boosey and
 Hawkes, 1955.
Gustav Mahler-Richard Strauss: Correspondence, 1888–1911. Ed. Herta
 Blaukopf. Trans. Edmund Jephcott. Chicago: University of
 Chicago Press, 1984.
Richard Strauss and Romain Rolland: Correspondence, Diary, and Essays. Ed.
 and trans. Rollo Myers. Berkeley: University of California Press,
 1968.
*A Working Friendship: The Correspondence between Richard Strauss and Hugo von
 Hofmannsthal.* Ed. Willi Schuh. Trans. Hans Hammelmann and
 Ewald Osers. Cambridge: Cambridge University Press, 1980.
*A Confidential Matter: The Letters of Richard Strauss and Stefan Zweig,
 1931–1935.* Ed. Willi Schuh. Trans. Max Knight. Berkeley:
 University of California Press, 1977.

Secondary Sources

Birkin, Kenneth. *"Friedenstag" and "Daphne": An Interpretive Study of the
 Literary and Dramatic Sources of Two Operas by Richard Strauss.* New
 York: Garland, 1989.
 Richard Strauss: Arabella. Cambridge: Cambridge University Press,
 1989.
Buelow, George and Donald Daviau. *The Ariadne auf Naxos of Hugo von*

Hofmannsthal and Richard Strauss. Chapel Hill, NC: University of North Carolina Press, 1975.

Del Mar, Norman. Richard Strauss: A Critical Commentary on His Life and Works. 2nd edn. 3 vols. Ithaca: Cornell University Press, 1986.

Finck, Henry T. Richard Strauss: The Man and His Work. Boston: Little Brown, 1917.

Forsyth, Karen. Ariadne auf Naxos by Hugo von Hofmannsthal and Richard Strauss: Its Genesis and Meaning. Oxford: Oxford University Press, 1995.

Gilliam, Bryan. Richard Strauss's Elektra. Oxford: Oxford University Press, 1991.

"Richard Strauss," The Nineteenth-Century Symphony. Ed. D. Kern Holoman. New York: Schirmer Books, 1997, pp. 345–68.

Gilliam, Bryan, ed. Richard Strauss and His World. Princeton, NJ: Princeton University Press, 1992.

Richard Strauss: New Perspectives on the Composer and His Work. Durham, NC: Duke University Press, 1992.

Hartmann, Rudolf. Richard Strauss: The Staging of his Operas and Ballets. Trans. Graham Davies. New York: Oxford University Press, 1981.

Jefferson, Alan. The Operas of Richard Strauss in Britain, 1910–1963. London: Putnam, 1963.

The Lieder of Richard Strauss. London: Cassell, 1971.

Richard Strauss. Newton Abbot: David and Charles, 1973.

Richard Strauss: Der Rosenkavalier. Cambridge: Cambridge University Press, 1986.

Kennedy, Michael. Strauss Tone Poems. London: BBC, 1984.

Richard Strauss. Revised edition. New York: Schirmer, 1996.

Kramer, Lawrence. "Culture and Musical Hermeneutics: The Salome Complex," Cambridge Opera Journal 2 (Nov. 1990), pp. 269–94.

"Fin-de-siècle Fantasies: Elektra, Degeneration and Sexual Science," Cambridge Opera Journal 5 (July 1993), pp. 141–65.

Krause, Ernst. Richard Strauss: The Man and His Work. Trans. John Coombs. Boston: Crescendo, 1969.

Mann, William. Richard Strauss: A Critical Study of the Operas. New York: Oxford University Press, 1966.

Murphy, Edward. "Tonal Organization in Five Strauss Tone Poems," The Music Review 44 (1983), pp. 223–33.

"Tonality and Form in Salome," *The Music Review* 50 (1989), pp. 215–30.

Newman, Ernest. *Richard Strauss*. London: John Lane, 1908.

Osborne, Charles. *The Complete Operas of Richard Strauss*. North Pomfret, VT: Trafalgar Square, 1988.

Pantle, Sherrill Hahn. *Die Frau ohne Schatten by Hugo von Hofmannsthal and Richard Strauss: An Analysis of Text, Music, and their Relationship*. Bern: P. Lang, 1978.

Peterson, Barbara. *Ton und Wort: The Lieder of Richard Strauss*. Ann Arbor, MI: UMI Press, 1979.

"Richard Strauss: A Lifetime of Lied Composition," *German Lieder in the Nineteenth Century*, ed. Rufus Hallmark. New York: Schirmer, 1996.

Puffett, Derrick, ed. *Richard Strauss: Salome*. Cambridge: Cambridge University Press, 1989.

Richard Strauss: Elektra. Cambridge: Cambridge University Press, 1990.

Schuh, Willi. *Richard Strauss: A Chronicle of the Early Years 1864–1898*. Trans. Mary Whittall. Cambridge: Cambridge University Press, 1982.

Strauss, Richard. *Recollection and Reflections*. Ed. Willi Schuh. Trans. L. J. Lawrence. London: Boosey and Hawkes, 1953.

Wilhelm, Kurt. *Richard Strauss: An Intimate Portrait*. Trans. Mary Whittall. London: Thames and Hudson, 1989.

Williamson, John. *Richard Strauss: Also sprach Zarathustra*. Cambridge: Cambridge University Press, 1993.

Youmans, Charles. "The Private Intellectual Context of Richard Strauss's *Also sprach Zarathustra*," *Nineteenth-Century Music* 22 (fall 1998), pp. 101–26.